D0986498

Walking Mom Home

Sharing the Blessings of This Life's Final Journey

MIRIAM MILLHAUSER CASTLE

A TARGUM PRESS BOOK

First published 2008
Copyright © 2008 by Miriam Millhauser Castle
ISBN 978-1-56871-466-0

All rights reserved

No part of this publication may be translated, reproduced, stored in a retrieval system, or transmitted in any form or by any means, electronic, mechanical, photocopying, recording, or otherwise, without prior permission in writing from both the copyright holder and the publisher.

Published by:
TARGUM PRESS, INC.
22700 W. Eleven Mile Rd.
Southfield, MI 48034
E-mail: targum@targum.com
Fax: 888-298-9992
www.targum.com

Distributed by:
FELDHEIM PUBLISHERS
208 Airport Executive Park
Nanuet, NY 10954

Printing plates by Frank, Jerusalem
Printed in Israel by Chish

Walking Mom Home is not intended to be a Halachic guide. Halachic issues require consultation on an individual basis with a *posek* well versed in such matters.

Rabbi CHAIM P. SCHEINBERG

Rosh Hayeshiva "TORAH ORE"

and Morah Hora'ah of Kiryat Mattersdorf

הרב חיים פינחס שיינברג

ראש ישיבת "תורה אור"

ומורה הוראה דקרית מטרסדורף

Words of Approbation

Eventually parents near the end of their lives and their adult children often see them through terminal illness, arrange their funerals and mourn their passing. The process can be intense and challenging, testing both parent and child. Many people fear the arrival of this time and suffer greatly when it arrives. Yet, in truth, it is a time that can offer enormous opportunity for growth and rectification -- a chance for parents and children to bond more deeply, to heal damaged or difficult relationships and to come closer to Hashem.

Rebbetzin Miriam Millhauser Castle has done a great service by sharing her remarkable experience seeing her mother (z"l) through the last year of life to her place of rest. Her book, Walking Mom Home, is an inspiring work that reflects great faith in Hashem, loving dedication to and honor of one's parent, and astute insights into life, death, mourning and grief. The experiences she describes demonstrate the elevated levels a soul can reach during its final *tikkun* in this world, and the many blessings for both parent and child in this final chapter.

Walking Mom Home is not intended to be a Halachic source and should not be viewed as one. Halachic issues pertaining to terminal illness require consultation on an individual basis with a *posek* well versed in such matters. This is a book with great wisdom and depth offering insight into how to make a time that otherwise might be considered sad and tragic, meaningful and rewarding. Anyone faced with these challenges, parent and child alike, will benefit from reading it.

רחוב פנים מאירות 2, ירושלים, ת.ד. 6979, טל. 537-1513 (02), ישראל

2 Panim Meirot St., Jerusalem, P.O.B. 6979, Tel. (02) 537-1513, Israel

Dedicated to my grandparents

Avraham (Albert) and Miriam (Marie Dreyfuss) Mühlhauser, z"l,
of Speyer, Germany

Yehudah (Judah) Baruch and Malka (Amalia Laufer) Rosner, z"l,
of Munich, Germany

who, along with other family members, were murdered in the concentration camps of World War II.

May their souls be bound in the Bond of Life and may their memories be for a blessing

With profound Thankfulness
To Hakadosh Baruch Hu

May I and all of klal Yisrael be privileged
to know who we are and what
You are asking of us.

May we have the faith and courage
to respond wholeheartedly.

Foreword
by HaRav Dovid Castle

abbi Yaakov said: This world is similar to a lobby before the World to Come; prepare yourself in the lobby so that you may enter the banquet hall" (*Avos* 4:21). The spiritual "banquet hall" is the true home of the soul. Every soul is sent into this world on a journey, with the mission to return home clean and pure. The early stages of the journey are marked by physical, emotional, intellectual and spiritual growth, when parents, though occupied with their own journeys, help and prepare their children for theirs. The end of life's journey is most crucial; the end of the soul's mission in this world. It is marked by physical decline, but also by the potential for emotional and spiritual growth which

HaRav Dovid Castle, *shlita*, is former *rom* and *menahel ruchani* of Yeshivah Gedolah Tiferes Avraham (ITRI) in Jerusalem and author of *To Live Among Friends: Laws and Ethics of Everyday Interactions*; *Living with the Sages: Rashi and Tosafists*; and *Darchei Dovid* (on *maseches Sotah*).

climaxes on the verge of death. It is written, *"Tosef rucham yigva'un, v'el afaram yashuvun* — When You retrieve their spirit they perish and return to the dust" (*Tehillim* 104:29). Rashi says the word *tosef* is related to *asaf*, gathering. Thus it means, "You gather in" or "You retrieve [their spirit]." The *Zohar* says that it is related to *tosif*, add or increase. Thus it also means, "You increase their spirit."

Shortly before death a person receives the greatest spiritual energy of his or her lifetime. This makes it possible to perceive and comprehend mysteries of the spiritual realm far beyond one's previous awareness. The final chapter of life is the final expression of the soul in this world. It is a chapter with much at stake, and is typically a challenging time. Ideally, children, though now in the midst of their own journeys, help their elderly parents through it. Unfortunately though, many parents and children find it difficult to come into sync with each other at this moment of destiny and often are uncomfortable talking about or planning for it.

Yet, for a child to care for a dying parent is a privilege of the highest order. And for a dying parent to be cared for by a loving child is a tremendous blessing. Rebbetzin Miriam Millhauser Castle and her mother, Gusti Rosner Millhauser, z"l, were fortunate enough to recognize the opportunity that Hashem was offering both of them when the senior Mrs. Millhauser was diagnosed with terminal cancer. But only after they had traveled the road to death for some time, did they realize just how miraculous the journey was and how they might be able to help others who would walk this road after them.

In *Walking Mom Home*, Rebbetzin Castle offers us the same depth, clarity, wisdom, and compassion that readers of her *Inner Torah* books have come to appreciate. She speaks openly, authentically, and directly about subjects that are too often whitewashed or glossed over. Whether writing of the impact of her mother's Holocaust past, the intricacies of navigating the mother–daughter relationship in adulthood, the challenges of being a caregiver, the realities of dying, the opportunities to grow and come closer to Hashem through loss and grief, or just the sheer joy of living a conscious and holy life whatever the circumstances, Rebbetzin Castle provides an honest, fresh, heartwarming perspective that will inspire and transform others in their *avodas Hashem*.

Acknowledgments

The writing of this book gives me another opportunity to thank my dear friends Diane Nemett and Abby Rosner for living this story with me. Their presence in my life is a huge blessing. They also were kind enough to read and give me their thoughts on the manuscript, which I greatly appreciate.

I'm enormously grateful to Rabbi and Rebbetzin Aharon Feldman, *shlita*, who were a tremendous source of support while I was caring for my mother, *z"l*, and who also read and commented on the manuscript. Rebbetzin Yocheved (Jackie) Wein, *z"l*, offered her love and encouragement throughout my stay in Baltimore and eagerly looked forward to reading this book. Sadly, she died before it was completed, leaving a void in my life and the lives of so many others. May her soul be bound in the Bond of Life and may her memory be for a blessing.

My heartfelt thanks and appreciation to Pnina Frank, who

after generously allowing me to use her paintings on the covers of my *Inner Torah* books, truly extended herself here by reading the manuscript and making a special painting for the cover of this book. My heartfelt thanks as well to the Scheller, Wealcatch, Mitnick and Segal families, Ahuvah Gray, Miriam Plotnikoff, Susi Kessler, Jane Lang, Paul Sprenger, Rosa Mitchell, Bess Salkin and Bobby Wolfe for their various and valuable contributions.

The staff of Targum Press worked as a team to bring this book to production. I greatly appreciate their effort and dedication. I also want to thank hospice for making it possible for me to continue to care for my mother, z"l, at home. The commitment of the hospice workers to making one's dying days livable is unequaled in any other health care setting. They deserve much gratitude and recognition.

My husband, who came into my life after my mother died, encouraged me throughout the writing of this book. He lovingly read each chapter and related deeply to my experience, coming to know my mother (and more about me) in the process. I am grateful beyond words for his rare combination of wisdom, strength, kindness, and sensitivity along with his unyielding commitment to Torah. May we be blessed to continue our work in service of Hashem together for many years.

Introduction

G-d gave my mother, Gusti Rosner Millhauser, *z"l*, and me, her daughter, an assignment. He asked us to walk through the door of cancer into the hall between worlds. And He asked us to wait there. To look head-on at life and what lies beyond. To join hands and solidify what had always been a committed and intense, though at times difficult, relationship. He encouraged us to find and name the strengths that lie buried within us. He gave us boundless resources from which to draw, each of us in our own right. And He gave us the inspiration to describe our experience, to offer it for whatever it is worth to help the many others who will walk into this same hall in the days and years to come.

These are the words I wrote while caring full-time for my mother who was dying. When first diagnosed with esophageal cancer the year before, she was told that she had a few weeks to a few months to live. Never wanting to endure a long, protracted illness as a prologue to death, my mother took the short prognosis in stride and readied herself to exit this world. Each morning she awoke took her somewhat by surprise, as the days stretched beyond the time allotted to her by the doctor who had pronounced her death sentence. She couldn't quite understand what she was still doing here.

I offered her the spiritual explanation that the soul leaves this world only when it has completed whatever it is that it came into this world to do. If she was still here, there must still be something her soul needed to do. She pondered that for a while but couldn't fathom what it might be that remained unfinished. "I just don't know what it is," she would say to me from time to time with a puzzled look on her face. There was something endearing just in the way she was giving herself over to the question. It was all part of the wonder of this time. The spiritual dimension of existence had slipped into our everyday conversation in a way it never had in the past. That was territory that I had always been more comfortable inhabiting than my mother. Now we were there together.

One day, a few weeks after we had first talked about this idea of completing the work of the soul, I said to her, "Maybe we're supposed to share everything we're learning as we go through this experience. Maybe we should write a book from our two vantage points that will help other people who are facing death or serving as caregivers for loved ones." She thought about that for a time and decided that it was a good idea. She had always wanted to die in her sleep, to avoid a long illness like my father, z"l, had suffered many years before. And yet, here she was, terminally ill, and finding the experience powerful, enriching, and meaningful in ways she could never have imagined. Maybe she really did need to share what she was learning before she could leave.

16

I took a yellow pad and a pen and sat down beside her. Together we began making a list of some of the ideas and events we wanted to talk about in the book. And, I wrote the words of introduction above. We both felt good about this new focus. We had spent months meeting the constant challenges of managing the illness and were in a place where, at least for the moment, things were steady. There was almost a false sense of settling into life again, with the massive changes brought about by the illness absorbed into our routine. That my mother no longer left the house, or even the upstairs floor where her bedroom, the bathroom and a recently improvised dining area were located, seemed almost natural to us. We had made a new life for ourselves in that limited space and we were busy living it. At least for the moment, the shadow of death had receded from its prominent place.

My mother's mind was completely sharp, but she could no longer write or read on her own because of side effects from the pain medication she was taking. We decided that the easiest thing to do would be for me to talk through ideas with her, try writing them up in draft, and then read them back to her to see if my words sufficiently captured her thoughts. That was *our* plan for moving forward.

G-d had a plan of His own. We never had a chance to work on the book again. Instead of moving us deeper into this new version of life we had created, G-d decided to open the gates and move my mother closer to death. Apparently the book had only needed to be conceived by the two of us together for her soul to be freed up to leave. Its birth, if there was to be one, would be my labor alone.

But that was all for another time and place. Our attention now was once again riveted on the physical and the changes that were happening that heralded the beginning of the end. We moved forward into these last days as we had all the days before, accepting G-d's decree, ready to do whatever the situation demanded of us, and bound by an enormous love that transcended anything we had ever experienced together before. My mother was going home. And I, her sole surviving daughter, was blessed to be able to walk her there.

Years after my mother's death, I finally decided to write this book about the journey of a lifetime — the journey to the door of the Next World that we will all one day take and that many of us will be privileged to participate in as caregivers for those we love.

May it be a source of comfort, guidance, laughter, and inspiration for those who read it. May it speak to mothers and daughters everywhere in whatever stage of life they find themselves. For this is not just a story of caring for a parent in her dying time or grieving after she's gone; it's a story of loving, growing, and reaping the fruits of relationship, of coming to know oneself in the cauldron of challenge, and of seeing oneself in the mirror of life's most primal connection.

Chapter One

I sat in the quiet of my Jerusalem apartment and pondered once again of what to do about my mother. She was in her eighties and lived alone in Baltimore, Maryland, the city in the United States where I had grown up. When I moved to Jerusalem years earlier I had been comforted by the fact that my sister lived ten minutes away from my mother. While I knew we would miss each other, I wasn't as concerned about her well-being. But in the intervening years, my sister, Malka bas Eliyahu, z"l, had died quite suddenly from a misdiagnosed illness. So now things were different.

My mother rallied remarkably well from the tragic loss of her daughter, accepting Hashem's will as she had so many other times in her challenging life. I had no questions about her emotional strength in the face of adversity. She had survived the Holocaust and the loss of her parents in concentration camps. She and I together had nursed my father, *z"l*, through a long and grueling bout with cancer ending with his death at the relatively young age of sixty-four. And she had fought her way back from her own almost fatal illness years earlier.

Still, now she was much older and for that reason alone, more vulnerable. The years ahead were likely to grow more difficult as she faced the inevitable effects of aging. Right now, though, she was healthy, vibrant, and more energetic than many people I knew half her age. Just the year before, she and I had gone on safari in Zimbabwe and then visited friends in Cape Town, South Africa. She had made the twenty-two hour trip on her own, meeting me in Johannesburg.

So I was confused. Do I go ahead with my plans to buy an apartment and settle permanently in Jerusalem or do I go back to the States to be closer to my mother in what, even under the best of circumstances, was approaching the end of her life. The alternative of her coming to live with me in Israel was not an option. Though I wanted to explore the possibility with her again, she previously had made clear that she wanted to remain in Baltimore. There she was independent, surrounded by friends, familiar with the environment, still able to drive, and comfortable living on her own in the house she had lived in for decades.

To uproot and start again in Israel where she didn't know the language, would have to make new friends, couldn't drive, and would, by necessity, be more dependent on me, didn't appeal to her at this point in life. I didn't blame her. The adjustment would have been enormous, even at an earlier stage in life. And the experts agreed. Almost all the professionals I heard speak on the subject cautioned children not to move their aged parents from familiar environs unnecessarily, and especially not to Israel where life is different and difficult even in the best of times.

To help me think more clearly about my decision, I attended lectures on *halachah* (Jewish law) relating to the obligations of children to parents in the later stages of life. Though always interesting, they were never definitive. It seemed that my situation, before the parent has or expresses a specific need for assistance, is a gray area left to the discretion of the child. Once the need is explicit, the obligation becomes clear. So for me, it was back to a matter of the heart. Jewish law was not going to decide this one for me.

Nor was my mother. Every time I asked her what she thought, she told me it was up to me; it was my decision and I had to do whatever I thought was best. That was the stance she almost always took in my adult life. Once we passed out of childhood and her sphere of responsibility as she saw it, my sister and I were on our own. She had made her views and values clear to us as children. How we chose to live our lives as adults was up to us. Even in this situation that so intimately involved her, she wouldn't offer an opinion. Though I could have surmised that she preferred to have me live near her, she might just as easily have wanted to see me settled in the land that would be my home long after she was gone. In truth, she probably felt pulls in both directions, as did I.

So the ball continued to bounce around my court. I went back and forth in my mind, sometimes preparing to use the waning days of my aliyah rights to bring my lift from America and settle in, and other times preparing to put my belongings from my Jerusalem apartment in storage and head to Baltimore. For reasons that I didn't yet understand, the decision felt pressing. I prayed that Hashem would show me the direction in which He wanted me to go. The mitzvah of honoring my mother seemed pitted against the mitzvah of settling the land. I wanted to do G-d's will; I just didn't know what it was.

Finally, my prayers were answered. While davening one day I understood clearly that I needed to close up shop in Jerusalem for a time and go to the States. I had no idea for how long or to what end. I just knew that the next step was to go and visit my mother, leaving open the question of when and whether I would return. I sensed that I would get more information once I was in the States and then would know what to do next from there. I would be able to see firsthand how things were with her and talk to her about how she envisioned this next phase of life unfolding. I finally realized that at this point I could only take the next step in front of me; I couldn't yet see the whole picture or make a definitive choice.

To facilitate that level of flexibility, I let my apartment go, put my things in storage and bought a plane ticket that allowed a return within one year. The day I boarded the plane for America, I didn't know when I would be coming back. I only prayed that Hashem would continue to guide me in making the right decisions each step along the way.

I arrived in Baltimore shortly before my mother's birthday. My sister and I never knew my mother's age precisely, though we knew that we had been born late in her life. She was of the generation that didn't share a lady's age as well as a host of other personal details. We had long ago given up prying and learned to accept the vagueness of years, especially since my mother seemed to defy the laws of aging anyway, continuing to move and to think like a younger person. The phenomenon was so noticeable that strangers would stop us on the street and ask her what her secret was, how she stayed so vital and vibrant at what was obviously an advanced age. My mother would just smile and refuse to take any credit, saying simply that it was the way G-d made her.

So here we were, preparing to celebrate her birthday of unknown years, with me doggedly trying to figure out whether she needed me by her side any time soon. Unlike me, my mother attributed no particular significance to this birthday — or this visit from me for that matter. Though she knew I had readied myself for a longer stay if necessary, she wasn't quite sure just what I was trying to base my decision on. As far as she was concerned, things were status quo until they were otherwise. And though she knew she was getting on in years, she still felt quite capable of managing on her own and didn't understand my sudden scrutiny of her circumstances. Valuing independence above all else, she was loathe to think that I was going to change course in my life for her sake. She couldn't accept such a thing, was all she kept saying when I tried out my various scenarios on her.

Still, I felt a clear and immediate need to attend to this question of my mother and me. I didn't know why. I just felt like Hashem was telling me that now was the time to pay attention to her, to factor her situation into my plans. Whether she was willing to face the issues of aging or not, they would come nonetheless. I wanted to be prepared, to know what we were doing and how we wanted to navigate through these waters when they were upon us. My mother wanted nothing of the sort. She always prayed that when her time came, Hashem would take her quickly — either in her sleep or "with her boots on" as she liked to say. She didn't want to give any energy to the scenario of prolonged incapacitation or any circumstance where she would actively need me, or anyone else for that matter, to take care of her.

23

So once again, I was thrown back on my own intuition. My mother was clear that she wanted to stay just where she was. She treasured her house and the memories of her husband and children it held for her. She had great friends and an active life filled with helping others and furthering her own education in all sorts of areas. She still traveled when she could, on various group excursions, and just generally relished every moment. Live each day to the fullest was her motto. On top of it, she seemed genuinely at ease. With all that she had endured there was a serenity about her that was palpable. She simply wasn't worried. "*Que sera sera*, what will be will be," she would often say, hoping it would help me, too, relax into the vast unknown that loomed ahead.

But I was not so easily placated. I still felt faced with a decision, made all the more clear by her certainty that she was staying put. Should I remain in Baltimore for a time and see how things unfold or should I take her at her word and return to Jerusalem? Again I debated. Again I prayed. And again Hashem answered my prayers. It became clear to me that I should get a temporary place to live nearby my mother. I was a little perplexed since she had no immediate need for my assistance. Still, I had come this far and arranged my life so that I could stay on if that seemed called for. I had asked and I had been answered. Understanding was a different story. Apparently, the reasons were not mine to know, at least not yet.

I immediately started to look for a place to live. I made a number of calls and arranged to see several apartments. On my way to one of them, I passed the apartment complex where my parents lived when I was born. It was not a place I had considered living. Yet, as I drove past, I felt as though the steering wheel of the car had been commandeered, and before I knew what was happening, the car was turned around and headed for the rental office. Next thing I knew I found myself inquiring about short-term rentals. There was one unit available. I went to look at it. It was perfect for my needs. I could have it for six months. It would be ready in four days. The rent was more reasonable than any of the other places. Hashem was not only telling me to stay, He was showing me where to live.

I began to wonder whether my sojourn in Baltimore was as much about my own *tikkun* (spiritual fixing) as about being there for my mother. I hadn't lived in Baltimore for many years. And now, of all the possible places to rent an apartment, I would be living in the same complex, indeed the same group of buildings, where my life began. There are no accidents. Everything is for a purpose. Maybe there was something that needed fixing in my soul that went all the way back to birth or the first years of my life. And maybe I needed to be in the actual physical space for that to happen. As a child, I hadn't lived a Torah-observant life. Perhaps I needed to return to my beginnings to have my return to Torah as an adult be complete, for it to truly penetrate the cells of my body.

Anyway, whatever the reason, I set about the task of preparing to move into my temporary quarters. My mother, meanwhile, had caught a cold as she did almost every year about this time, and she was taking it easy. I looked in on her periodically as I gathered the essentials together and, on Sunday, began to move a few things to the apartment. That night I was awakened by a strange sound. It took me a minute to place the noise, and then I realized that there was something wrong with my mother's breathing. I jumped up and ran into her room. She seemed almost out of it. I sat her up, placed my hands on her back and, with energy work, tried to help ease the constriction in her breath. All the while I talked to her, until slowly she seemed to come around, was more aware of her surroundings and able to breathe a little easier.

By now it was early morning and I called my mother's doctor. She had us come to the office, examined my mother, x-rayed her lungs, and announced that she had a serious case of pneumonia in both lungs and would have to be hospitalized immediately. She made the arrangements with the hospital while I transported my mother there. Everything happened very fast and we were both quite stunned at the sudden turn of events. But we didn't have a chance to ruminate for long. No sooner was she settled in her room in the hospital and receiving oxygen treatments that a new complication developed. Her heart went into an irregular pattern. Next thing we knew we were rushing her bed down the hospital corridor to the intensive care unit, the doctor on one side of the bed and me on the other.

At one point the doctor, looking terribly sad and troubled, said to me, "She might not make it out of this, you know; after all, she's eighty-eight years old." This woman had been my mother's doctor for years and was very fond of her. I knew it was hard for her to get those words out, yet at the time the most stunning announcement for me was that my mother was eighty-eight! "Eighty-eight" I exclaimed and I'm sure the doctor thought I was a little off to be reacting to the age rather than the dire prognosis. Still, I couldn't contain my amazement. It didn't seem possible that someone so lively, sharp, and energetic could be eighty-eight, let alone that she could be on the verge of death. I think I was in shock.

The next few weeks were touch and go. My mother stayed in intensive care and I stayed with her, either in her room or in a little cubicle the hospital reserved for visiting family members to spend the night. Respiratory therapists, cardiac and pulmonary specialists, and a wonderful cadre of nurses tended to her. Through it all she kept on smiling and trying her best to make things pleasant for all of her caregivers. We had some long soulful talks, including about her age which I had to let her know had been disclosed along the way. Pesach came and we made a beautiful bedside Seder, aided by the Jewish community that supplied all our needs and the hospital staff, that went out of its way to be respectful of our tradition. At times it almost seemed surrealistic. We had gone from an academic discussion of the possibility that one day she would need help to an immediate need in the face of a life-threatening condition. Neither one of us knew what hit us; we just faced each day and somehow made it through.

She was a champion, doing all the breathing exercises and, when the time came, getting herself up and walking again with very little rehabilitation. She was anxious to go home once she was clear that it was not yet her time to leave this world. And she knew that was possible only with my assistance. The Torah teaches that Hashem provides the cure before the illness; and that's exactly what we were seeing. The doctor told us it would take about four or five months once she was released from the hospital to fully get her strength back. Not only had I been there, right in the room next to her at her time of initial need, but I had already made the arrangements to stay six months. It felt like a miracle. And we both couldn't have been more grateful.

Chapter Two

Something had happened during this month in the hospital beyond my mother's recovery. Something had happened between us. The super-independent stance that my mother had adopted early in life as a young girl in Germany, and that had stood her in good stead through a host of trials and tribulations, had softened. She had needed me and I had been there for her. The need had been non-negotiable. Not like the emotional challenges she had faced, where she could will her way to the other side. This time the need was physical. There were things she could not do until she got her strength back. Grocery shopping, preparing meals, laundry, and a host of other household chores that she had always done for herself were temporarily out of her reach. For a time she was so weak that she couldn't even sign her name.

She had to surrender. She had to learn how to receive after a lifetime of giving. None of this was easy for her. I talked with her often about it, as an opportunity provided by Hashem to help her develop these long under-utilized aspects of herself. Torah teaches us balance. Giving and receiving must be in proper measure. To be locked into one mode or the other limits the soul's ability to manifest fully. In truth, receiving can be its own form of giving, I would explain to her. Rather than seeing it as a loss of independence, she could see it as giving others the opportunity to do for her and reap the enormous rewards that come from serving those we love. She knew how good it made her feel to help other people. She did it all the time. Just think, I would tell her, how good other people, including me, are going to feel finally being able to help you.

She heard the words and tried hard to take them in, but I could see she was still chafing under the bit of her new feelings of vulnerability. That was the problem, really. On the receiving end we experience greater vulnerability than we do on the giving end, where it at least appears that we are in control. Now she wasn't in control. I appreciated how difficult and frightening that was, but I still felt it was a blessing in disguise. She would experience aspects of herself that she didn't know, and I, too, would have an opportunity to relate with those hard-to-reach parts of her. And let's face it, control is an illusion anyway. Ultimately, we are all vulnerable to Hashem's will, we just don't think about it most of the time — until something happens and reminds us just how little control we really have.

In the weeks following her return home from the hospital she had no choice but to let me do for her, and she accepted relatively graciously. We even joked about how she could get used to being waited on. But I could see that her intention was to be up and about on her own strength as soon as humanly possible. She worked hard to recover her lung capacity, using the contraption the hospital provided when she was discharged.

It was a plastic thing that you had to breathe into forcefully enough to get a little ball to go above a certain line. She puffed away. With her other activities, she tried to do just a tiny bit more each day, while taking care not to overexert herself.

Her friends, who had inundated her with cards and flowers throughout her stay at the hospital, couldn't have been happier when she came home. They began bringing all sorts of culinary treats and an assortment of gifts to cheer and encourage her. It was actually a very sweet time. It was made even sweeter by the fact that she knew that she was on the road to recovery. The doctor had made it clear that it was just a matter of time before she would be as good as new. The end of the summer was her target date. Until then, she figured, she would be careful to curtail her usually busy schedule. She postponed a visit to relatives on the West Coast that had been scheduled for July until she was stronger. She didn't want to take any chances and invite a relapse. One bout with pneumonia was enough.

Within about a month she felt secure enough for me to move into my apartment. I still grocery shopped and came over every day, but she resumed meal preparation and some light chores. Her steady stream of visitors kept her company and she was able once again to read and listen to music, her favorite pastimes under any circumstances. Her old self was slowly coming back. I was happy about that for her sake. The only problem was that I could feel some of her "independent armor" coming back at the same time. That was too bad. I felt the little opening we had crafted together closing somewhat. But I understood what was happening and had long ago surrendered to my mother's ways, understanding that she did what she did out of her own very real needs and not to hurt or distance herself from me.

As I thought more about it I understood even more deeply

why she would need to shore herself up in some of her old ways at that moment. She was in a vulnerable place in life. She was advanced in years and had just endured a life-threatening illness where she essentially had to turn her well-being over to a staff of doctors, something she never liked. My mother tried hard never to need doctors or medicine. She only took vitamins and did everything in her power to keep herself healthy. She ate well, exercised, and even had learned to meditate in order to bring down her blood pressure, which had shot up after my sister's death. She had never been even a pound overweight, fluctuating between 101 and 104 pounds on her 5'2" frame for her entire life other than during pregnancies. It made sense that she needed to regain her sense of control now that the worst of this illness was behind her.

Slowly, we settled into a new routine as she resumed responsibility for herself. I began work on a book I had long been hoping to write and returned to my healing practice and Torah studies. It was the first time in my adult life that my mother and I had lived in the same city, let alone five minutes from each other. Before I moved to Israel I had lived in Washington D.C. Although only an hour away, it was enough to require advance planning and a chunk of time before we got together. Now we were able to drop by on the spur of the moment and visit each other for a few minutes, or do a few errands together, or have a quick bite to eat whenever we wanted. It was great. We both loved it and I commented often on how lucky I felt to have this opportunity, though I wouldn't have guessed in a thousand years that I ever would live in Baltimore again.

Several times a week, my mother would come to my apartment for a treatment. I did energy work and would schedule appointments for her as I did my other clients. She loved the sessions. They were relaxing, rejuvenating, and strengthening for her. And she was a great client. Very energy sensitive, she could always report on where the energy was moving in her body and how my interventions were affecting it. It was a pleasure to work with her. She also had the capacity to let the energy carry her to deep realms. Sometimes I would look at her on the table and feel that she was miles away. At times it seemed almost like she was drifting out of this world and I would wonder whether she was exploring the terrain of death with its bright light and higher vibration energy field. It concerned me, but at the same time it didn't have a sense of immediacy. Her recovery had been exceptional. She looked better than she ever had, with a veritable glow around her. When I mentioned it to her she quipped, "G-d's shining me up before He takes me."

It wasn't unusual for my mother to talk casually about death. She had been doing it for years. Not afraid to meet her Maker when the time came, she just didn't want to suffer prolonged illness as my father had. She had executed a living will and health-care power of attorney years before, making clear her end-of-life preferences. She would tell me just to make a bonfire after she was gone, as a way of saying I didn't need to get bogged down in all the things that were in the house that she hadn't been able to part with in her lifetime. "They gave me pleasure," she would say; "they don't have to mean anything to you." I used to joke with her, too, telling her only half in jest not to buy any more "stuff," since I would be the one stuck getting rid of it all as I had with my sister, *a"h*. She laughingly told her friends about my admonition and even made a half-hearted attempt to comply. Against this backdrop, the comment about G-d shining her up before He took her didn't seem remarkable, even if she had just survived a very close call.

After the treatments, she would sometimes stay for dinner. She was a good sport, trying the different greens and soy dishes that were the mainstay of my then-vegetarian diet. She had never veered from a standard three meals a day, often having chicken or meat as part of her evening meal. She always had two cups of coffee in the morning and never stopped eating butter or anything else she liked that suddenly showed up on the experts' "bad for you" lists. And no dinner was complete for her without dessert. Granted, one cookie, one piece of cake, or one scoop of ice cream was enough. She never knew from binges. But she did pretty much eat exactly what she wanted her whole lifetime. The thing she was a stickler about was water. She drank eight glasses a day without fail. That and the vitamins were her prescription for good health and, for the most part, they had worked.

As much as anything else, we were enjoying our many differences during this time together. We had a good chance to see how each other lived on a regular and up-close basis. We not only ate differently and kept house differently and cultivated different kinds of relationships with our friends, but we lived our Judaism differently. She grew up in a Torah-observant home in Germany and shifted to Conservative Judaism when she came to the United States as a young adult. I grew up in a Conservative Jewish home and became Torah observant as an adult.

That we were able to maintain mutual respect and appreciation for each other in the face of such enormous lifestyle differences was a wonder to many of my mother's friends, and apparently they would comment to her about it. After years of struggle, we were both deeply gratified to have such a good relationship. It felt like the fruits of a lifetime of labor, of wrestling with each other, trying to influence and change each other. Until at some point — I'm not sure either one of us could identify precisely when — acceptance set in and we were on our way to a whole new world. We talked easily and laughed often with each other. We sought each other's opinions on day-to-day questions and happily headed off on excursions together. We were each finally free to be who we were and able to enjoy each other from there.

What made it difficult was that I didn't know what I was doing long-term. The lease on my apartment required two months' notice to avoid an automatic renewal. That meant I had to decide whether come September I would return to Israel or stay on in Baltimore for another period of time. My life in Israel was basically on hold. Friends and clients from there continued to call regularly, understanding that my mother's illness had prolonged my stay. Now that my mother was better, they were wondering when I planned to return.

Here it was again. The same question. This time it loomed on the other side of an experience where my mother very clearly had needed me and, thanks to Hashem's guidance, I had been there for her. Now what? Should I stay, should I go, should I split the year between the two places? Again I didn't know. Again I debated. I looked at condominiums, thinking that if I had a small apartment in both cities I could come and go more easily. I wouldn't be constrained by leases to specific time periods here and there. At one point I consulted a well-respected *rav* in the community, who told me I could go to Israel. Still I felt torn. I convinced the rental office to give me additional time to make my decision. I didn't know what the outside parameters were any more. Would I be living in Baltimore indefinitely? Would I ever make it back to Israel? Again I turned to Hashem. I davened. I asked for guidance on this same question for the third time. And again I got it. Stay in Baltimore. Renew the lease for another six months. Don't worry far into the future. Just take this next step, make this next six-month commitment.

Again I didn't understand. Why was Hashem telling me to stay when my mother was fine? Why six more months? What was the purpose of these repeated short-term plans? Why wasn't Hashem helping me to craft a longer-term solution? Even my efforts to find a condo had fallen flat, as had my efforts to locate a suitable apartment in Jerusalem when I had tried the previous year. Although I have a substantial capacity for living in the moment, the tentativeness of this arrangement was a strain. After all, I had come six months earlier with one suitcase. I had to purchase clothing and other things that I already had in storage in Jerusalem. It was a hard situation to relax into, but I did the best I could. At least I had certainty for another six months. I didn't have to put any more energy into making the decision. That was a relief in and of itself.

I returned my focus to the book I was writing and life resumed its steady rhythm. Aside from having time with my mother and a quiet place to write, I discovered another silver lining to my stay in Baltimore. That summer, while I was busy debating whether to stay or go, Rabbi and Rebbetzin Aharon Feldman, *shlita*, came to live in Baltimore. The Feldmans had lived in Jerusalem for more than forty years, had eight exceptional children there and more than sixty grandchildren. Yet Rabbi Feldman had responded to the call to serve as *rosh yeshivah* of Ner Israel Rabbinical College in Baltimore. Having gotten to know the Feldmans when I lived in Jerusalem, I, along with everyone else in Baltimore who knew them, was thrilled that they were here. I looked forward to spending time with Rebbetzin Feldman and helping in any way that I could as they got settled in their new home.

By now it was almost Rosh HaShanah. I hadn't spent the

chaggim in the States for years. My mother would be attending the synagogue to which she had belonged since coming to Baltimore in the early fifties. She sat in the same seat every year and was herself a source of comfort and continuity to many of the congregants. She also had long-standing traditions with several of her friends to join them for the holiday meals. The shul was Conservative and so not suitable for me, and the friends with whom she ate didn't keep strictly kosher so I couldn't join her there, either. Instead, I went to be with the Feldmans for the *chaggim*. Though my mother and I wouldn't be celebrating together, we felt very connected to each other going into this New Year and understood why each of us was where she was. That we chose to pray and eat in different settings had nothing whatsoever to do with the depth of our love for each other. We were clearer about that now than we had ever been.

After the holidays, I resumed writing in earnest. I was deep into the book by then and hoped to complete it by the end of the year. Between the writing and everything else I was doing, my life was full if still not fully rooted. I had put the question of the future out of my mind for the time being, knowing that I didn't have to make another decision until February, two months before my renewed lease was up. My mother, meanwhile, had resumed her full schedule. She was not only fully recovered but seemed miraculously to have even more zest and energy than she had before.

Chapter Three

*U*nfortunately, we had only a few weeks at full tilt before my mother was stricken with a terrible toothache. Next thing we knew she needed a root canal. There was a complication and for reasons that we didn't understand, the pain didn't go away. The doctors loaded her with antibiotics and other medications to which she started having strong reactions. It was a mess. Nobody seemed to have a handle on precisely what the problem was. They tried changing the medication. Meanwhile, she started complaining of a tight feeling in her lower ribs. We researched endlessly on the computer. She tried to keep up with her schedule even though she was uncomfortable, but before long it got to be too much for her. Finally they got to the bottom of her problem with the tooth but by then she was having what seemed to be a bad case of indigestion that she thought was brought on by all the medication.

The night of November 5, Ahuvah Gray, a good friend of mine from Jerusalem, was in Baltimore to speak about the book she had just published. My mother had promised to go to a farewell dinner that night for a friend who was leaving for Florida, but she also wanted to hear Ahuvah speak. We arranged that I would pick her up at the restaurant where the dinner was held and take her to the synagogue where Ahuvah was speaking. I was so happy to have my mother sitting beside me that night. Rebbetzin Feldman was also there and I had a chance to introduce the two of them, which was a great joy. At the last moment, Rebbetzin Feldman unexpectedly asked me to give the opening remarks. As I stood on the bimah and looked out over this sea of women, I saw my mother sitting right in the middle. It was one of those nights when she was truly glowing and I couldn't have been happier.

But it was also a night when her condition seemed to have taken a turn for the worse. She told me after she got home that she hadn't been able to swallow her chicken at the dinner. She could eat the soft vegetables but not much else. I could also see as she sat beside me that she was in pain, though she did her best to hide her grimaces.

The next day she talked to her doctor again, who prescribed medication for acid reflux, which all of her symptoms, including the difficulty swallowing, seemed to suggest. The doctor told her it might take a couple of weeks to feel the benefit and told her to call again in three weeks to let her know how she was. In the meantime she should eat soft foods that were easy to swallow.

The weeks went by, but instead of getting better she was getting worse. By Thanksgiving, her condition had gotten so bad that she could only take liquids. I researched acid reflux and learned just how bad it could get. I tried making her nutritious broths to keep up her strength. But it was clear that some other kind of help was needed. She was losing weight and feeling more pain by the day.

The Monday after Thanksgiving weekend we went in to see the doctor, who told my mother she would have to have an endoscopy and scheduled it for the next day. In that procedure the gastroenterologist would put her to sleep, insert a tube down her esophagus and be able to see exactly what was going on. At the time of our visit to the doctor that Monday I still believed we were dealing with a severe case of acid reflux. I had brought the results of all my research with me to the doctor's office, but she politely ignored me every time I tried to raise the subject. She busied herself getting the endoscopy scheduled and telling my mother how to prepare for it. At that point we both wanted the test and to know what was happening. We didn't have any clue what the possibilities were. We just knew that whatever had been tried until now hadn't worked and, therefore, the next step had to be taken.

I took my mother home and returned to my apartment, planning to pick her up early the next morning and take her for the test at a local hospital. That night I put the finishing touches on the draft of my manuscript and, for the first time, printed out a copy of the complete book. My mother had enjoyed the excerpts I read to her along the way and had been asking me when she would be able to read the whole manuscript. Now here it finally was. I didn't think too much about the fact that it was the eve of her endoscopy. It just seemed like another procedure we would have to go through to get to the bottom of whatever was wrong and then, once again, she would be on the mend. At the time, she was convinced that somehow all the antibiotics she had taken for her tooth problem had irritated the lining of her esophagus. She went over that sequence of events time and again in her head, wishing that she had been more assertive about not taking so much medication that she knew disagreed with her.

With all that in mind, and the satisfaction of completing the draft of the book, I laid down to sleep. But sleep never came. Something else happened and I'm still not sure I can explain it. My body felt different somehow. I felt like I was in some sort of altered state, one I had never experienced before. I asked aloud what was happening. I got up and walked around. I knew something out of the ordinary was going on but I didn't know what. At some point, and I can't say exactly when, I knew that whatever was happening to me had something to do with my mother. And then again, a little later on, without knowing how, I knew that something bad was about to occur. And finally, some time in the early hours of the morning, I knew she was going to die. It was as real as if I had just received a telephone call informing me of the news. By that time I was almost out of my skin. I had spent the entire night awake with the news of what awaited my mother and me slowly penetrating my consciousness.

My first thought, of course, was that she wasn't going to make it out of the endoscopy, which, like any procedure in which you're put to sleep, carries that risk. I went to pick her up with my heart aching and fear in every cell of my body. On the way to her house I stopped at a grocery store that was open at that early hour to bring her a little surprise. I saw balloons with expressions of good cheer on them. Reaching for one that said, "Get well soon," I pulled back my hand. A sense of dread waved over me. I already knew she wasn't going to get well. Instead I bought the one that said, "Hope you're feeling better." When I got to her house, she was in good spirits, glad to be getting this test over with and anxious to begin the proper treatment. She was already thinking about what she was going to eat when swallowing was no longer a problem. I wanted to cry just looking at her but I didn't. I pretended to be upbeat and optimistic right along with her.

We didn't have to wait long after we got to the hospital. She barely had enough time to fill out a bevy of forms before her name was called. I was allowed in to help her prepare for the procedure. I stood at the foot of her bed as she waited for the nurse to insert the needle necessary to put her to sleep. Needles were always hard for her because she had small veins and, invariably, all but the very best ended up butchering her before they got in. So she was nervous about that. To relax her, I held her feet in my hands and gently massaged them. Later she told me she could feel the love in my fingers as I did that. Fortunately, the nurse turned out to be extremely skillful. Before my mother knew what was happening, she drifted off to sleep. Taking a last look at her sweet face, I went back out to the waiting room.

For the next forty-five minutes I went back and forth between the waiting room and the ladies' room about six times. In between, I prayed. Somehow it didn't seem possible that this was happening. My mother's health had been perfect just the month before. And, until the night before, it had never even occurred to me that my mother's death was imminent. I was so sure that she still had time ahead of her. My energy was directed toward finding a way to dovetail our lives for this next period so that I could be there for her. I certainly wasn't thinking about saying goodbye. Yet the premonition the night before had been clear. Everything was about to change.

The nurse came out, told me that the procedure was

finished and that I could go back to see my mother. I felt an enormous wave of relief crash over me and raced back to her cubicle. She was very groggy but smiling, obviously happy to be on the other side of the ordeal. She told me how wonderful the doctor and nurses had been, thanking them at the same time. Meanwhile, the doctor motioned to me to step out with him. We moved a few feet away from the curtain behind which my mother lay. "It doesn't look good," were the first words out of his mouth. I was stunned. The only risk I had entertained was that she wouldn't survive the procedure. Now, here she was, awake and smiling and he's telling me it doesn't look good. Before I could say anything he started to describe the mass he had seen in her esophagus that, at that point, included much of the medication she had been taking that hadn't made it down. I asked if we could move further away. I didn't want my mother to overhear bits and pieces of this conversation.

People walked by us in the hall but I was only vaguely aware of them. What was he saying? Finally he used the words, "malignant growth." "We'll only know for sure when we get the biopsy back but it seems pretty certain..." The room began to spin and I realized I was starting to faint. A nurse quickly brought a chair, put a cold washcloth on my forehead, and told me to put my head down. The doctor squatted next to me. "I'm sorry," he said and continued on with his description of what he had found and how he had pushed down some of the material that had gotten stuck so it would be easier for her to eat. I tried to rally and concentrate on what he was saying but it was hard. I was hearing a death sentence. He knew it and so did I. We decided it didn't make sense to tell my mother until the biopsy results were back and the diagnosis was definitive. "Maybe we'll be surprised," he said, probably trying to alleviate the pain he saw in my face or throw out a thin ray of hope to justify the delay in informing my mother. "Today is Tuesday. I'll put a rush on it and try to have the results by Friday. Call my office and make an appointment for then. I think it's better to give her the news in person." With those words, the doctor walked away and I was left to get myself together enough to face my mother.

I slipped into the ladies' room, cried for a minute or two, washed my face and made my way back to my mother's bed. She was still out of it enough not to pick up that anything was wrong. I helped her dress, went to get the car, and took her home. Lucky for me, she was still feeling the effects of the anesthesia when we got home and wanted only to get in bed and sleep. While she slept I alternated between tears and panic. I wondered what I would say to her. Dare I hope that he was wrong, that the biopsy would come back negative? If I hadn't had my experience the previous night, that option would have been easier. But the combination of my nocturnal premonition and the doctor's words left me little room to hide.

My mother awoke about two hours later, just as happy as could be. She felt better, probably because the doctor had pushed through some of the blockage so she had more space in her esophagus again and less pressure. It was clear that she thought the worst was behind her. She wanted to hear the CD of old tunes a friend of mine had recorded in New York and just recently sent to us. It broke my heart to see her sitting up in bed, joyfully singing along with songs from her past. The contrast between our two realities at that moment was overwhelming.

Finally, late in the afternoon, she asked me if the doctor had told me anything about what was wrong. It was the moment I was dreading. I told her he had seen a mass of some sort that had embedded in it a lot of fragments from all the medication she taken the last month. The tissue was heaped up and irritated. He had taken a biopsy and hoped to have the results by Friday. I didn't let on that he was almost positive that it was malignant. This was enough for her to digest. The word biopsy alone signaled the possibility of malignancy. She knew that. She chose to talk again about how terrible all the medicine for her tooth had been and how sensitive she was to medication. She still hung on to that as the cause of this current problem. She even continued to berate herself for not being more careful and more assertive with the endodontist.

That night she felt well enough to stay on her own so I went home. It gave me a chance to ask my close friend Diane to come over and be with me as I let the full impact of what was happening hit. Between sobs I cried out to Hashem, "I'm not ready, I'm not ready for this." By "this," I meant everything. I wasn't ready for my mother to die. I wasn't ready for the grueling course that cancer takes. I knew it only too well from my experience with my father who had suffered tremendously. There is nothing more painful to watch than the slow demise of a person you adore. I knew that. I wasn't ready for any of it. "No," I cried out, knowing even as the words left my mouth that Hashem had issued His decree and there was likely no way out. Still, I prayed and begged.

By the next day I realized that Hashem had given me a gift. He had given me time to prepare myself and get myself together before my mother got hit with the truth. I had a few days to myself to release a lot of the initial feelings, so that when the time came, I could be there fully for her. I deeply needed to allow myself time to feel and to take in the full significance of what was happening. That was my way.

My mother, on the other hand, was coping as she coped with everything else. At times in my life I called it denial and at other times eternal optimism. Whatever it was, over the years I had moved from denigrating to respecting it. In her book, everything was fine until facing the alternative was absolutely unavoidable — and even then she usually found a way to make it fine again very quickly. She believed strongly in *"bashert,"* that everything that happens is exactly the way G-d wants it to be, and there's no use getting too upset or railing against even the worst of occurrences for long. She was a master at taking things in stride and moving forward. Granted, in this situation she didn't know the worst of it, as I did. Still, she knew that cancer was a distinct possibility. I had been slipping the word in more and more in order to prepare her for Friday. By Thursday, I had told her that the doctor said it might be a malignant tumor and that we would know for sure by Friday. I didn't want her to be totally blind-sighted when she went in there.

For a brief moment on Thursday evening she let in what I was saying and her spirits sunk. But she rallied quickly and by Friday was hopeful she would get a good report, as she put it. Our appointment was at noon. The doctor had made time for us during his lunch hour. The gastroenterologist and my mother's internist are part of the same practice. So we entered the waiting room where we had come so many times before. How different this time felt. I knew that when we walked out of there, life would never be the same again. I tried not to cry. The doctor's secretary was a very sweet woman who, as soon as she heard my mother's German accent, began telling us about her mother who was also German and had died the previous summer. She had tears in her eyes as she talked, obviously still feeling the pain of her loss. My mother, as she always did, leaped in to comfort her. I couldn't help but feel the poignancy of the moment, knowing that soon I would likely be the one talking about her with tears in my eyes.

Now that we were in the offices, it was hard to wait any longer to hear her fate, our fate. My mother, who disliked waiting under the best of circumstances, was getting antsy. So was I. I had told my two close friends, Diane and Abby, that if the news were bad I would be staying at my mother's house that night. I didn't know if I would be able to call them before Shabbos, but they would know from where I was what the results were. I didn't want my mother to be alone with a difficult diagnosis even for a second. I never wanted her to wake up alone in the night again, if indeed she had cancer. I had packed a small bag with my things and put it in the trunk of the car before I picked her up. I was ready, at least on the physical level.

Finally our turn came. We entered the doctor's office and immediately my mother commented on how beautiful the décor was. It was. I could see he was somewhat taken aback by her obviously genuine focus on his furnishings. He tried to catch my eye but it was hard for me to look directly at him, knowing he would be broadcasting the news with a single glance. Instead, I kept my focus on my mother as she sat down on the chair in front of his desk. I sat down beside her. "I hope you have a good report for me," she said with her usual smile on her face. "I'm afraid I don't," the doctor said. I kept my eyes on my mother. At first her expression didn't change; then I saw a flash of distress cross her face. Watching her receive this news felt like it was going to be even harder than receiving it myself. I still didn't look at the doctor. He began to describe the very large malignant tumor that was clogging her esophagus.

He used a diagram as he talked. On it he drew an image of the blockage immediately above the entrance to her stomach. It was an 8-centimeter squamous cell tumor, which, in his opinion, had been growing there for some time. The tumor growth was too extensive for surgery, which, anyway, would not have been recommended at her age. There was no possibility of cure; only various palliative measures that might make it easier for her to eat.

My mother used the time he was talking to retrieve her composure from some very deep place inside herself. The look of distress had only lasted an instant and then she had forced herself to rally. It was a display of inner strength that I will never forget. Her immediate response was to say, "I don't want any heroics; I just don't want to suffer." In those few words, she let him know that she understood what he was telling her. My own memory of those agonizing minutes in his office is blurred. At some point I know that he volunteered a prediction that she had somewhere between a few weeks and a few months to live. I was in shock. This had all happened so unexpectedly and so fast. How could we be so close to the end?

The standard treatments of radiation and chemotherapy were not options in my mother's case for a variety of reasons that he laid out for us. By then, though, my mother was barely listening. Those were not options she would have entertained even if the doctor had recommended them. Not at her age. Not after she had witnessed what my father, *z"l*, had endured in his fight against cancer many years earlier. She wanted no part of it. Her reaction was the same to his suggestion of a feeding tube inserted in her stomach that would allow her to be nourished even if the tumor blocked her esophagus entirely. Her wish was to die naturally, with as little medical intervention as possible. Her living will and health care power of attorney made that wish abundantly clear and she had reiterated it herself every chance she had.

I had no question about her preference in the face of terminal illness. Yet one palliative measure the doctor mentioned caught my attention. He talked about the possibility of inserting a stent that would open the esophagus and allow for more normal eating. This could both prolong life and make it more comfortable. That option seemed like it was at least worth further thought, even though my mother dismissed it along with everything else. First, though, we had to digest the news we had just been given. Then we could think about whether there was anything that could be done to ease the way.

By now we were both numb. Sensing that neither of us was taking in his words any longer, the doctor brought the meeting to a close, saying something peculiar about how I would always remember her or something to that effect, which I wasn't ready to hear and my mother, fortunately, didn't hear, at least as far as I could tell. I ushered her out quickly, before he could say anything else that would jar our sensibilities even more than they already had been. With one hand on my mother's arm and the other clutching the notes I had taken in the doctor's office, I guided my mother to the elevator. We were dazed. I don't remember much from the ride home except that at one point my mother said quietly, almost to herself, "I'll never drive this road again to my class." Remarkably, it was the first and last statement I ever heard her utter bemoaning her fate.

As soon as we got back to my mother's house we had to quickly prepare for Shabbos that was about to begin. My mother sat at the kitchen table while I prepared our meal. She began to review the sequence of events that had gotten her to this point. She went back over the root canal and all its complications, the pain she had felt in her chest, the difficulty swallowing. It had all happened in a matter of weeks. That was the most stunning part. She kept talking about how she had been in New York less than a month ago and had felt fine. How could all this have happened so quickly? She wondered whether the pneumonia had something to do with it. I chimed in often, filling in dates and symptoms, sharing her utter disbelief at what we had just been told. How could it be?

We would review the litany of events many times over the next few days. It was our way of digesting the enormity of what we had been told. Less than a month earlier, my mother had been enthusiastically and fully living her life and happily planning for the future. In fact, just six weeks earlier my mother had gotten a full checkup from her primary physician — her last follow-up visit after the pneumonia. The doctor gave her a clean bill of health and told her to come back in six months. She even had her little card scheduling her next doctor's visit for April 15. We had celebrated her outstanding recovery and her return to twice-yearly doctor's visits — which was more than enough in her book. To go from there to a death sentence that could be executed as early as within a few weeks and at best a few months was more than either of us could fathom. And so we repeatedly told each other the story, trying to take it in.

It was significant for us that we went from receiving the diagnosis directly into Shabbos. For the next twenty-five hours we wouldn't be answering the phone, listening to the radio or doing anything other than praying, eating, learning the Torah portion for that week, talking to each other, and resting. We were on our own with Hashem. And that felt like a blessing. The comfort and peace of Shabbos were exactly what we needed as we grappled with the huge turn in the road we had just been asked to make. While my mother had often said she wasn't afraid to die, she was so fully immersed in life and so lively and energetic that it always felt very remote. Some day, of course, she would die, but aside from the pneumonia scare, it never seemed like it would be any time soon. Yet now, on very short notice, she was being called home.

49

Chapter Four

ortunately, both of us trusted Hashem. My mother always said that each of us is born with a little number next to our name and when our time is up, that's it. Even when faced with the devastating loss of her own daughter, she never questioned Hashem's will. "It was her time," she would often say, and didn't try to question or argue with G-d. For my part, I trusted that everything Hashem does is for the good. That didn't stop me from crying out bitterly when my sister died and questioning often the missed diagnosis Hashem chose as the way to take her out of this world. But underneath all my distress was rock-solid knowledge that whether or not I could fathom His ways, they were merciful and in furtherance of some bigger picture that I could not see.

The first night my mother had been aware of difficulty swallowing was November 5, the night of her friend's going away party and my friend's book talk. The endoscopy was performed on November 27. By the night of November 30 we had her terminal diagnosis. The speed of it all had us reeling. Then, as if on cue, and before we could catch our breath, her body upped the level of pain. The vise she had complained of feeling around her torso seemed to tighten and the Tylenol she had been taking no longer was enough. By the next day, stronger medication was needed.

This was the beginning of what turned out to be our greatest challenge — managing the pain. My mother was highly sensitive to just about every medication. Whatever relief a medicine brought on the pain front was usually accompanied by a host of side effects that were every bit as bad as, if not worse than, the original problem. Our initiation into this dilemma was swift. Within three days after beginning the pain medication, her body was totally impacted. The impaction itself became even more agonizing than the tumor pain and we were forced to go to the emergency room of the local hospital for relief. There we faced a six-hour wait before we were even seen. It was incredible. Even though my mother was elderly and obviously in enormous pain and discomfort, and even though her doctor called repeatedly, we had to wait. Sitting across from us was a man with kidney stones. It was a toss-up between my mother and him as to who was in greater distress.

Finally our turn came. We wheeled my mother back into one of the cubicles, where we were met by a truly wonderful nurse practitioner named Terry and another nurse named Mike. They couldn't have been kinder, gentler, or more caring. Our hours of waiting evaporated under their tender, loving care. First they wanted an X-ray to make sure there was no obstruction. Once they saw there was none they knew that the culprit was the pain medication. Mike was the one who actually performed the procedure. He treated her with great respect and sensitivity and was able to put her at ease in a way that can only be described as artful. Very quickly we came to learn just why he was so gifted. Both his wife and daughter suffered from illnesses that required frequent intestinal interventions, so for him it was natural and almost second nature. His attitude was contagious, turning what could have been a horrific experience into an almost pleasant, albeit uncomfortable, one.

Meanwhile, Terry took it upon herself to look for an alternative pain medication that wouldn't cause the same problem. She came up with the Duragesic patch, which is applied to the body and releases medicine slowly into the blood stream over a period of three days. She put the patch on my mother that night, hoping it would not only have fewer side effects but would also give her more consistent pain relief. She was right. The patch proved to be a valuable part of our pain management program throughout my mother's illness. We considered it the silver lining in our first crisis. Through the ordeal of the impaction, Hashem led us to an approach to handling the pain that we might not have reached for some time. For that, and for our encounter with these two angels, Terry and Mike, we felt grateful. Hashem was with us.

We left the hospital at 2:00 in the morning. When we got home my mother was full of energy and ready for a cup of tea. We sat at the kitchen table, cups in hand, like nothing had happened. It was one of many demonstrations of my mother's extraordinary resilience. My friend Diane, who was with us, couldn't believe it. My mother managed to emerge from the ordeal looking great and smiling. Really, what had astounded Diane the most was when, after the procedure was finished, my mother stood up on the narrow ledge at the side of the procedure table, balanced on one leg, and gracefully put on her stockings. Diane watched in amazement. My mother was not only flexible and dexterous, she was totally composed once her problem had been addressed.

By now we were six days into our new life, with one crisis under our belts. Events were unfolding fast. My mother's capacity to swallow seemed to diminish almost daily. I was pureeing foods finer and finer and even still we had our share of choking and gagging. We both had to get a grip very quickly in order to endure those episodes. The key was not to panic. I would gently massage the area and try to release the block. My mother would try to breathe and cough up whatever she could. In between she would try sips of ginger ale to induce a good burp and hopefully dislodge whatever was stuck. Sometimes it would take hours, after which my mother usually was too exhausted to eat anything else. She was just happy to have relief from the pressure and pain of whatever had gotten stuck. I usually lost my appetite too. It was a terrifying thing to witness and I could only offer limited assistance. We both had to maintain enormous faith each time it happened and trust that, with Hashem's help, we could get through it.

We fell into working as a team almost instantly. Whatever happened, whatever was needed, we were in this together. Thankfully, we both were very resourceful, relatively creative, and long on patience. We would need all those traits and then some in the days ahead. There are no guidebooks to the many vicissitudes of major illness. Essentially, you're on your own, not knowing what will happen next. No sooner do you cobble together a solution to one problem than the next one hits. A state of vigilance takes hold inside. You're always ready, always on alert. In our case, we had the added pressure of not knowing from one day to the next whether the tumor would grow in such a way that the esophagus would be blocked entirely. The first sip and first bite of the day were tinged with tension. Would it go down?

In addition to managing the increasingly worsening symptoms, I felt we had to research the array of possible treatments. Perhaps there was something outside of conventional surgery, chemo, and radiation that might be helpful. The doctor had already mentioned the stent. My own brief research had revealed some other newer therapies as well, in particular a photo-dynamic laser treatment that could shrink the tumor and create more space in the esophagus. We at least had to know what all the options were. Then my mother could make an informed choice about what, if anything, she wanted to do.

My close friends, Abby and Diane, jumped into gear to try to get information. Diane is an osteopath and physical therapist with lots of connections in the medical world. She quickly zeroed in on the top esophageal expert in town, a doctor at Johns Hopkins Hospital. Meanwhile, Abby searched the Internet and learned more about the stent, photo-dynamic laser therapy and some other approaches to keeping the esophagus open. The disease itself could not be cured. The tumor would continue to grow and, in all likelihood, spread to other parts of the body if it hadn't done so already. The best we could hope for was to find a way to prevent the tumor from totally blocking the esophagus and preventing any intake of nourishment. In the process, it was possible that the tumor might be reduced in size or its growth slowed, but progression of the disease was inevitable.

We scheduled an appointment with my mother's primary-care doctor a week after the initial diagnosis. Originally she had planned to join us in the meeting with the specialist the week before but hadn't been able to make it. After all their years together, my mother very much wanted her input and opinion. She knew my mother well and understood her sensitivity to medication as well as her outlook on life. And they genuinely liked each other. The bout with pneumonia had only brought them closer as they reveled in what was really a rather spectacular recovery. Now we were in entirely different territory. It was no longer a matter of recovery, but rather finding ways to minimize suffering during the ordeal that lay ahead. They were both such fighters; it had to be sad for them to acknowledge that they were approaching the end of the road together.

At least that's what I thought. But when I accompanied my mother into her doctor's office I witnessed a different sort of exchange. After the usual exchange of pleasantries, they both acknowledged the new reality with only the briefest of comments. I don't remember my mother's words but I remember her doctor saying, "It stinks," and going on from there. They were both realists. The situation was what it was and apparently, in both of their views, there was no sense bemoaning it. We quickly got down to business. I had a list of questions on everything from medications to diet to next steps and we went through them all. By this point, my mother had basically ceded control of pragmatics to me. She would just reiterate that she didn't want any heroics and she didn't want to suffer. Yet she also didn't want to be overly medicated. She was leery of the side effects and also wanted to stay sharp mentally for as long as she possibly could. Fortunately, her doctor was sensitive to her desires and ready to work with us to try to accomplish them. That, in and of itself, gave my mother some peace of mind.

We left the doctor's office with a plan to meet with the esophageal expert from Hopkins as soon as possible and with a prescription for the Duragesic patch to which the emergency room nurse practitioner had introduced us. Together with the doctor we had decided to use the lowest level patch supplemented by liquid extra-strength Tylenol to manage the pain. As for the expert, my mother was willing to hear what she had to say, perhaps for my sake as much as anything else. In her own mind, she wasn't particularly motivated to find ways to prolong her life under these conditions. Had there been a chance of a cure, she would have pulled out all the stops and tried whatever she could. It was clear that her love of life was undiminished in that sense. But given that the disease was already far along and only going to worsen, she didn't want to fill whatever days she had left with medical interventions which, in the end, would not save her. She preferred to face her death head-on, to accept that G-d was calling her, and to answer that call with as much dignity and courage as she could.

The doctor who initially diagnosed the cancer told me later how much he admired the way my mother accepted her fate. "Not everyone is as willing as she is to accept when their time has come and to face it so directly and bravely," he said. He also told me "that it is often the patient's desire to try everything and anything — even if there is little or no likelihood of success — and that influences a doctor's recommendations. For many patients it is easier to keep taking treatments that are ineffective than to face their own demise. And doctors oblige. Because for many doctors it is also easier to keep doing all sorts of things than to admit that there is nothing within their power that can help. It is almost as though doctor and patient collude to avoid the reality of death."

Not my mother. She was eighty-eight years old. She felt she had lived a full and satisfying life. And she would have been happy to continue living that life. But now that she had a terminal illness she knew that was not meant to be. So now she had to ready herself to die. As we drove home from the doctor's office for the second Friday in a row, I could see that she had already begun to make the shift. She was adjusting to her new circumstances, letting go of plans for the future that only a week and a half ago had still been on the table. The new car she had ordered months earlier, that miraculously had been delayed in delivery, was now canceled. Her tickets to various performances in the weeks ahead had been given away. She had begun to tell her friends and to try to infuse them with her own sense of peace about the verdict she had been handed. As I listened to her I couldn't help but feel that in the process of reassuring them she also was reassuring herself. "It's G-d's will," she would say. "Everyone is born with a little number next to their name and this is mine." "It's time," she would say. "I've lived a full life; I'm ready to go." This was her refrain in one form or another. She neither questioned nor complained. She seemed to simply accept her fate and turn her sights in the direction of leaving this world.

I had a much harder time. I was so not ready to let her go. One night as we sat together going through some papers, she put her head down on the desk. She seemed so weary and fragile at that moment. "Don't go," I heard myself say. "Please don't go yet; I'm not ready." All she could answer was, "I can't promise anything." I felt an undercurrent of fear in my body. Yet on the surface I was able to appear relatively calm and definitely in control. I knew the responsibility was mine and, more than anything else, I wanted my mother to be able to relax and rest into knowing that she was in capable hands. For that to happen, I had to keep it together and stay on top of everything that needed to be done.

One of those things was food preparation. I had called the American Cancer Society and gotten some materials from them. But mostly it seemed to be a matter of trial and error. Many of the recipes in the cancer society pamphlets were either too sweet or the wrong consistency. Pureeing certain foods was fine and others seemed to be rendered inedible by the process. The various liquid supplements were unpleasant. Some foods, even when they were the right consistency and tasted okay, would still get stuck or cause gagging. I started using little poached egg dishes to make small servings of lots of different things, hoping that one would hit the spot. Anyway, the portions had to be small as my mother had little appetite. Large amounts of food would have overwhelmed her before she even started.

And then there was the constant bitter taste that seemed to stay in my mother's mouth no matter what we tried. One day, we remembered an anise-flavored sucking candy from long ago. Thinking that perhaps that would work, I set out to try and find some. After striking out at all the candy stores, I tried a mail-order place that specialized in things from the past. Sure enough, they were able to locate it and send it to us. It worked for about a day and then that too began to taste bad.

Next I bought a juicer and tried making a host of fresh fruit and vegetable juices. It got to the point where my mother never knew what concoction was coming next. I tried just about every combination I could think of to find something that would be pleasing to her palate. Fortunately, we were able to laugh a lot as we tried all these different things. Our laughter and irreverence saved us time and again as we struggled with all the little challenges of our circumstances and the big challenge of where we were headed.

The other big preoccupation for my mother, aside from eating, was making sure that I knew all the ins and outs of her affairs. She was a meticulous record keeper and wanted to show me everything. For my part, I found it hard to concentrate on administrative details in the face of everything that was going on. We would sit together at her desk reviewing papers and ledgers and going through files as she tried to give over the intricacies of her system. I always wanted to cut to the bottom line and get on to something else. Here, too, we would manage a good laugh as we faced how different we were from each other in this realm. As much as I wanted to ignore this aspect of things, I sensed that it was important to my mother to feel that the sense of order that she cherished was being maintained. As I slowly took over responsibility, I tried to do things as she had, so she could feel the continuity and relax. As I did so, I realized that I was also affording her a sense of ongoing control. Her mind was still sharp and she knew exactly what needed to be done. It was just that she couldn't physically do it anymore, so I did it for her.

This attitude proved important to both my mother and me. It allowed her to maintain her self-respect and dignity; she very much felt herself the master of her ship until the very end. I simply acted as her hands and feet in those areas where she couldn't do for herself. I didn't try to impose myself or my ways. Honoring her in this way was actually freeing for me. Instead of challenging her idiosyncrasies, I made myself an agent to carry them out. Quite simply, I gave her the space to be herself fully and freely without questioning, advising, criticizing, or second-guessing. I felt that it was hard enough for an independent woman like her to find herself physically dependent on someone else. That was enough of a loss in and of itself. To lose autonomy and freedom of choice at the same time would make it unbearable. All her life my mother had feared becoming dependent. She never wanted to be a burden to anyone, least of all her children. If anything, that attitude had made her a little too self-reliant in my view. There was almost nothing anyone could do for her. In some ways, I was grateful to finally have the opportunity to do for her, to be close to her in these ways. And I wanted to do it in a way that would be least intrusive.

We were helped in the process of getting affairs in order by a book called *Supportive Cancer Care*. Diane had picked it up for me, thinking that it might have some good ideas on the diet and nutrition questions that were coming up. While it wasn't all that helpful on the food front, it had a chapter called "Your legacy of love" which was very informative. It contained forms and questionnaires designed to help cancer patients address various areas of importance, including advance medical directives, location and content of records, family information, funeral arrangements and obituary, and distribution of assets. While we had covered a lot of territory on our own before we got the book, it jogged our thinking on a number of issues we hadn't focused on before. And it made it very easy. We could go down the checklist and respond to the items one by one. It helped us gain a sense of where we were in the process. My mother, the consummate organizer, was so pleased with this book that she immediately told all her friends about it, urging them to use it to get their affairs in order, too. Some actually did.

My mother had a will, advance medical directive and power of attorney executed years before she became ill. What the book did was to help us get a handle on the more amorphous aspects. By the time we went through all of the forms we felt like we were in pretty good shape. In the process, we also went through the contents of my mother's safe-deposit box. It was filled with all sorts of forgotten treasures which we spread out on the kitchen table. My mother had a chance to tell me the history of some of the pieces of jewelry and other items we found in there. We even found an old pocket watch of my father's that my mother took to wearing around her neck, and one of his rings.

When her finger became too swollen to wear her wedding band, she put it on a chain along with the ring we had found and wore that as well. They gave her tremendous strength and comfort. That day at the kitchen table was a sweet time that became a precious memory. To do the same task alone after she was gone would have been sad and burdensome.

By the end of the following week, we had an appointment with the Hopkins specialist. Again it was on a Friday. Diane drove us downtown to Hopkins and came with us into the meeting. We didn't know when we would have the chance to talk to the doctor again, so I wanted to make sure we covered all our bases. Between us, Diane and I could take notes and ask questions and, hopefully, find out everything we needed to know. When we went to register at the reception desk, the receptionist took one look at my mother and exclaimed, "You are a beautiful woman." And indeed she was. Small, elegantly dressed, and with that glow around her face, she truly lit up the room even at that early hour of the morning. Nobody would have ever guessed that she was on the verge of death.

The doctor was a nice woman who took great care to explain what options were available to patients with esophageal tumors. Much depended on the stage of the cancer and the position of the tumor in the wall of the esophagus, neither of which were known to her in my mother's case. More tests would be needed, specifically a CT exam and a swallowing test. The CT would reveal if the cancer had metastasized to other parts of the body and the degree of penetration of the esophagus. The swallowing test would show if there was any other swallowing problem and if there was a leak between the esophagus and any other organ. Once the doctor had that information, she would know whether my mother was a candidate for photo–dynamic laser therapy.

This therapy involves injecting a photosensitive drug that localizes in all cells but more in the cancer cells. Two days later, an endoscopy is performed with a laser. The laser activates the drug and causes a photochemical reaction that destroys tumor cells and, in turn, increases the opening. There is usually discomfort for several days after the treatment, due to inflammation. For four to six weeks after the treatment, the patient is light-sensitive and can't go outside in the sun without special clothing. Even in the house, sunlight has to be kept to a minimum. The goal is to be able to eat more normally and therefore feel stronger and have a better quality of life for whatever period of time remains. There is also a chance of slightly extended survival.

The other option is a stent. This involves running a guide wire across the tumor and slipping a stent over the tumor to create an opening. It allows for normal eating relatively quickly. Patients experience variable degrees of pain induced by the stent. Some tolerate it easily and some have chest discomfort. The difficulty is that once it is inserted, it can't be removed. There is also a chance that it could slip, be displaced, or get overgrown, though such things happen only rarely.

As the doctor went through her explanations my mother seemed to drift off into her own reverie. Diane and I asked lots of questions; my mother asked none. She repeated her aversion to heroics, but she agreed to at least get the tests necessary to determine what, if any, treatment might be suitable for her. Not wanting to waste time, we tried to schedule the tests that same day. They were able to fit her in for the CT scan but not for the swallowing test. We would have to return on Monday for that.

We left the doctor's office and made our way to the waiting area for CT exams. Because they were doing us a favor by squeezing us in, we had no idea how long we would have to wait. Another woman doctor met us with some forms my mother was asked to complete. Because a dye was to be injected, there were certain risks involved that had to be explained. The doctor did so very sweetly and then brought my mother two large containers of chalky liquid to drink, in preparation for the CT. Everyone in the waiting area was nursing one or more of these drinks, but for my mother, who had difficulty swallowing, it was an enormous challenge. First she thought she wouldn't be able to do it. Seeing her dismay, the doctor quickly decided that given my mother's small size, one container would be enough. That helped.

But what helped even more were two brothers sitting across from us. They seemed to be old-timers in the CT department. Somewhere in their late sixties or early seventies, they both had cancer. But they were anything but typical cancer patients; they were more like a comedy team. They joked that between them they had had enough body parts removed to make another person. They told my mother how they had decided to move in together after the younger brother was diagnosed. One of them was divorced, the other had lost his wife, and they both had a few children. But they decided that they could best handle their circumstances if they were together. So the younger brother sold his house in New York and moved into his older brother's home in the countryside in New Jersey. Their children took turns helping them out when they needed something. One had actually typed up their "itinerary" for their visit to Hopkins that day, with all of their different appointments and tests listed by time and location. They proudly showed it to us. In between trips like this one to Hopkins, doctor visits, and treatments, they were building a boat in their backyard which they hoped one day to be able to sail.

All of that, in and of itself, seemed amazing. But then they proceeded to banter back and forth about who had to undergo which procedure first, who had more chemo and radiation, whose surgery was the most difficult, and all sorts of other things. In one way, they sounded like any two brothers, each trying to make himself more important than the other. The incredible thing was, that it was their cancer treatments and experiences that had become their currency of self-importance, not to mention the fact that they were on in years, so that it all seemed slightly absurd. But it did the trick. Their *shtick* distracted and entertained my mother so that she managed to down the drink she had been given — which was probably their intention to begin with. Also, their optimism was infectious. They obviously were not going to let their cancer prevent them from living and laughing and even planning their sailing voyage. After the heavy meeting with the specialist, being with them was a relief. My mother went into her CT exam laughing, and we were once again convinced that Hashem had sent a pair of angels to ease our way.

After the scan we went home to prepare for Shabbos. For the third Friday in a row we were heading into Shabbos straight from a doctor's appointment with a lot to digest. While I seemed encouraged by what we had heard from the specialist, my mother was more skeptical. She wasn't particularly interested in viewing the video that the doctor had given us about photo-dynamic laser therapy. And she didn't seem to want to talk much about that treatment or the stent. Still, the subject came up during Shabbos and I tried to put in my two cents about how I thought the laser therapy in particular might be helpful. I think I had already concluded that there was no way she was going to get the stent, with all its potential complications and irreversibility. Mainly I was hopeful that we could improve her capacity to eat, remove the stress of choking, and make mealtimes more enjoyable.

I ended up looking at the video by myself after Shabbos. It tried to put a good face on the procedure but there was no getting around the days of inflammation and discomfort immediately after the treatment and the extreme precaution that had to be taken for another four to six weeks after that to minimize exposure to sunlight. Walking around outside all bundled up in special protective clothing and sitting in the house with the shades drawn tight just couldn't be presented in a very appealing way, though the makers of the video had obviously tried. I realized that it was probably just as well that my mother hadn't wanted to see it. I wasn't at all sure it would have helped persuade her.

As it turned out, the Hopkins specialist was planning a vacation in early January. If we wanted to go ahead with the laser treatments we would have to schedule them immediately, in order to get all of the necessary appointments in before she left. With that deadline looming over our heads, my mother somehow tentatively agreed that I could make the appointments. I set up the four sessions at the only times the doctor had available. They were to extend from the end of December to the end of the first week in January. That gave my mother another two weeks to live with her decision before treatment would actually begin. In retrospect, I'm sure that's the only reason she agreed to make the appointments; she knew she still had time to get out if she changed her mind.

The next day, Sunday, my mother had a ticket to the opera. The performance was one in a series of operas for which she and several friends had purchased tickets well before any of this had happened. While she had already given most of her season tickets for concerts and plays to other friends, opera was by far her favorite music and some part of her obviously was hoping she would still be able to go. I offered to take her and wait for her outside the concert hall in case she got too tired or uncomfortable and wanted to leave. At first she wouldn't hear of it. But I kept telling her that I was happy to read in the lobby while she enjoyed herself inside. That amazed her but, ultimately, she agreed to the arrangement and off we went.

I got such pleasure from seeing her once again out doing something she loved. The last few weeks had been unbearably hard, with the diagnosis, doctors appointments, tests, pain, and emergency room visit. The opera seemed like a little light in the darkness for her. I was happy to make it possible for her to attend and she was enormously grateful, thanking me over and over again for waiting there for her.

She even seemed to understand that I actually enjoyed having the time to read and that it wasn't a burden to wait for her. This was not a small thing in the context of our relationship. During this time of heightened togetherness, we were actually having a chance to individuate even more. Years ago, my mother and I used to try to convince each other of the value and benefit of the things we each found valuable and beneficial. It had been hard for both of us to fully accept that we had very different values and tastes. Instead, we both tried to promote the things we liked and make them more important somehow than things that were high on the other's agenda. We had long since given up on doing that. But it was in the months following the pneumonia that we actually had a chance to experience, while in close proximity, each of us living her own life and doing the things we each liked to do. We recognized, even more than we had before, how far we had come in terms of accepting our differences. Now, though, we were actually living together and, because of the circumstances, spending all of our time together. It was no longer a question of each of us doing whatever we pleased and coming together to share common ground. We were together all of the time, so it was easier to fall into old patterns.

The opera was a quick test of where we were holding. At first, my mother tried to convince me how wonderful opera was and how much I would enjoy it. I knew that she was speaking from an old groove, and I was able to gently remind her that it wasn't for me. She quickly regained her footing on healthier ground, glad that I could appreciate her love of opera. She accepted that I received great pleasure from helping her to do something she liked and that I actually preferred to spend the time reading. No judgment running in either direction. When she came out of the performance all enthusiastic, with some reference to what I had missed, I realized it was just her way of telling me that she would have liked to share something that she loved so much with me. And that was perfectly fine. We were standing together in our separate truths, even in such an insignificant matter, and it felt good.

The next day we had to go back to Hopkins for a swallowing test. Its purpose was to see if there were any other swallowing problems other than those caused by the tumor, and to determine whether there were leaks between the esophagus and any other organ. This test involved drinking barium and recording the swallowing from the time the liquid entered the mouth until it reached the stomach. It turned out to be relatively simple, and no other problems were found. So, there was no obstacle to going ahead with the laser therapy — at least in theory. What was going on in my mother's head was another story. She wasn't saying much about it all. She had mentioned the option almost in passing to a few friends. One had a son who was an oncologist and also quite close with my mother. He took it upon himself to come over to talk to her in person and to try to convince her to do some kind of treatment. He held out hope that she would be able to eat normally again and would generally have a better quality of life for the time she had left.

Untreated, her esophagus might soon close up entirely, making it impossible even to take liquid nourishment. She would literally starve to death. That prospect loomed large over me, making the first sip of every morning a frightening experience, as I waited to see if there was still enough of an opening to allow whatever she was drinking to go down. When it did, I would silently breathe a sigh of relief.

Usually, we started the day with an instant breakfast drink. I had decided to join her in that meal, at least, and would bring two steaming mugs of it up to the bedroom. At other times I was faced with the uncomfortable situation of eating food that was no longer an option for her while she consumed yet more liquid or pureed fare. It was hard for me to eat under those circumstances, but I knew how much she wanted us to have meals together. I took to making meat and chicken soups for her, that yielded a very nourishing and tasty broth, so that she would have something that felt more substantial. As I was vegetarian at the time, that took some getting used to. Again, it became a source of pleasure for me as I saw how much she enjoyed them.

And, at some point, we also discovered ice cream. It stemmed the tide of weight loss for her and was another thing that we could both enjoy eating. So I stocked up on coffee, her favorite flavor, and it quickly became one of our staples. We had it several times a day, usually with a little actual coffee poured over it. By some miracle, or maybe simply by virtue of all the stress, I actually lost weight on that ice-cream diet. It never happened before or again.

Meanwhile, in the midst of all these appointments and tests, came the holiday of Chanukah. My mother had always lit the menorah she had brought with her from Germany and said the *berachos* from a siddur given to her as a gift by one of her Hebrew school teachers when she was a child there. This year was no exception. She asked me to set up candles for her as I prepared my oil lights. As I did so I couldn't help but think that this was the last year we would be lighting together. It felt unbearable. To know so clearly that this was the end, to watch for the last time this woman who had given birth to me light the *chanukiah* that had belonged to her parents and hold the siddur she had used as a little girl. These were the images on which I had been raised and soon I would never see them again. How could I ever make these moments significant enough, how could I absorb the absolute finality of what was taking place? Neither of us mentioned the obvious. We lit as we had so many times in the past. We sang "Haneirot Halalu" and "Maoz Tzur." We took a few photographs. And then we hugged. And the tears that came to our eyes said it all.

Two days after the swallowing test we got the results of the CT. The words I later found noted on my mother's calendar for that day sum up her reaction — "Bad news but relief to know the truth. All will be well with G–d's help." The CT showed that the cancer had already metastasized. There were lesions in the liver and nodes in the abdomen. For the most part they were small, a few millimeters, but there were many of them. The primary tumor in the esophagus was now ten centimeters, with the smallest opening now one centimeter, still enough for pureed foods and definitely for liquids. But there was no guarantee how long that opening would remain.

My heart sunk when I heard the news. When we had been thinking of the photo–laser therapy, we had assumed that her only problem was in the esophagus and that this was potentially a way to address it. Now we knew that her condition was worse than we had thought. It might be the cancer in her liver or even her stomach that would be the immediate cause of her death. Would she still be interested in a treatment that only addressed the esophageal tumor?

I didn't have to wait long to find out. We had arranged a telephone meeting with her primary-care doctor the next day, to go over the CT results and discuss what to do. We sat in the same room, holding two different phones so that we could both talk. The doctor reviewed the results with us, confirming what we had learned the day before. And she offered her thought that the laser therapy might still be beneficial, just to maintain a passageway in the esophagus. My mother listened quietly to her; I asked a few questions. And then my mother shared her decision. She had said nothing about it to me or to any of her friends before this moment. Apparently, she felt a certain confidence in her relationship with this doctor, who had seen her through the recent bout of pneumonia and the various blood pressure and heart scares she had suffered after my sister's death. For she told her, in a very quiet and calm voice, that she had thought about it long and hard and had decided not to take any treatment. Her doctor, living up to the confidence my mother had placed in her, offered no resistance. My mother went on to explain that she didn't want to spend her last days going to doctors and hospitals for treatment that anyway would not cure her or even prolong her life in any significant way. She said again that she had lived a long and satisfying life, that she was ready to go, and that she preferred to let the illness take its course rather than intervene.

The doctor accepted her decision and went on to talk about a question that had come up in relation to one of the pain medications. I sat there somewhat stunned. Though I shouldn't have been surprised that once she heard there were metastases my mother would opt for no treatment, I was still taken aback. First of all, this meant that we wouldn't get any relief from the tension around getting nourishment. She had already refused a feeding tube, so we were left with whatever she would be able to take by mouth. And that was totally dependent on whether an opening of sufficient size remained in her esophagus. The prospect of living with that unknown on a daily basis for an unknown period of time was daunting. Of course, my mother probably was still thinking about the prognosis she had heard when first diagnosed, of a few weeks to a few months to live. In some ways, she was banking on it. And by now she was already three weeks into that time period.

Secondly, her decision meant that we would be facing death head-on now, with no measures at all to delay its onset or ease the way other than pain medication. It asked me to join her in her courageous stance. And I had to admit, at least to myself, that I was frightened. Having already cared for my father and my sister in their dying days, I knew how crisis-driven this time could be. I knew that I would have to be constantly alert, creative in responding to emergencies, persistent in getting medical help if needed, sensitive to even subtle changes and generally focused on a myriad of physical details, any one of which could prove significant at any time.

Chapter Five

In these first few weeks since the diagnosis, I had taken on the challenge, but with the treatment option still at least in potential. Now that avenue was closed. We would be walking straight to death's door by whatever route Hashem decided to take us. It required enormous faith, which my mother seemed to have naturally. For my part, while my faith was strong, I was also wrestling with fear. I felt it in my body. I was afraid of all the things that might happen physically, all the possible emergencies with which we might be confronted and that I might not be able to handle. And I was afraid of her dying, of being permanently separated from this woman from whose body I had emerged and with whom I had been bound for a lifetime.

The mother-daughter bond by definition is strong. In Holocaust families, which mine was, it tends to be even stronger. My father's early death bound us closer again. And my sister's death some years later deepened the connection even more. We had been through a lot together. Our relationship, while not always easy, was strong and committed. We had always been an integral part of each other's lives, a significant factor in each other's equations even as we lived very separate and independent lives. And now that was about to end. She was preparing to leave this world. My job for the moment was to help her go. And then I would need to go on.

This was all crystallized in that moment when she declined treatment. There was nowhere left to hide, nothing to focus on other than the steady march toward the end. I was a little hurt that she hadn't shared her decision with me first, before telling the doctor. It felt like something so private, so personal. Why would she deal with it in a conference call with the doctor? After all, I was the one who was most affected by it and would feel its impact most strongly.

In retrospect, I think it was this very fact that influenced her to do it the way she did. I think she knew on some level that she was disappointing me, that I would have liked her to try something. And while she would have liked to be responsive to me if she could have, to do so in this case would have violated her own deepest instincts. I think that by informing me through the conversation with the doctor she was trying to shore up my faith in the decision and to avoid a lot of discussion that she knew would not convince her to change her mind. She was trying to handle it in a way that she thought would be easiest on both of us. That much I now understand. Still, I felt a sting at the time.

We were both quiet for a while after that call. A little later I canceled the appointments we had made for the laser therapy. Finally, that night we talked about where we were.

One of the things on my mind was the funeral arrangements. I remembered that when my sister had died some years before, I had been faced with the unpleasant task of arranging for her burial at the same time as I was dealing with the shock and pain of her death. While my mother's situation was different because she already had a plot beside my father and my sister hadn't had one, no other arrangements were in place. There was still the coffin to select and the other details of burial to be worked out. I even remembered back many years when we had had to do the same thing for my father, *z"l*. Each time it had been difficult and unpleasant at a moment that was already hard enough by virtue of the death itself. I wanted to avoid going through it again. So I suggested to my mother that I go to the funeral home and make all the necessary arrangements now, while she was still here. That way I could come back from the task that I so dreaded and she would be there. I could hug and kiss her and tell her all about it. I wouldn't feel like I was doing it alone and I wouldn't be trying to cope with the reality of her death at the same time. She thought that was a great idea so I made an appointment for the middle of the following week.

Hospice was the other subject we focused on that night. Now that she had declined all curative measures and was heading into the end of life, it made sense to get hospice involved. Hospice services would make it easier for me to take care of my mother at home, where she wished to stay, and hopefully make it possible for her to die at home, which was also her wish. We agreed that I would call the local hospice and find out what we needed to do to sign up. We both understood the enormity of this step. Hospice services are only provided for people who are terminally ill, with less than six months to live. The whole idea of hospice is to help people die in peace, comfort, and dignity. Most of the care is provided in the home, with an in-patient facility available only if needed for intensive medical intervention or some other unusual circumstance.

I felt again the low-level fear in my body. We were talking in such a matter-of-fact way about something so enormous. My mother was dying. We were thinking together about what she would need during her last days and about her funeral. It was almost surrealistic. I ached from anticipation of the loss. And I worried about what horrors might lay in store for us along the way. From that night on, I prayed to G-d to please take her to Him like a mother gathers her baby to her breast. I begged Him to grant her a peaceful passage, to spare her and me the type of trauma that had marked both my father's and sister's deaths in different ways. I felt our fate in His hands more starkly than I ever had before. He would decide how these days and weeks would unfold, what would happen to my mother, and how she would ultimately be taken from this world. I was totally powerless to influence the events that were to come. I just had to be prepared to do whatever was asked of me by the circumstances. It was that simple — and that hard.

I lay in the bed beside hers that night, feeling deeply the turn in the road we had just taken. We were no longer digesting the diagnosis, taking tests, or exploring treatment options; we were getting ready for death. I had decided to sleep in the other bed in her room so I would always be by her side if anything happened or she needed anything in the night. I had made that decision the moment the doctor told her she had only a short time to live. I didn't want her to be alone with that reality. I wanted to be with her, to give her whatever I could, to do whatever she needed. She had embarked on a journey and I wanted her to feel me firmly by her side. Our roles had reversed. I was now the one taking care of her, tending to her needs, providing support and comfort. We had come full circle. The torch was about to be passed. But I wasn't sure I was ready to take it.

I listened to the sound of her breath as she slept. She was still alive, still in the world with me. We could still talk and laugh. We could still share memories of my father, my sister, and all sorts of things that had happened in our family over the years. We held these people and events in our hearts. By talking about them we continued to give them reality in a more tangible way than one person alone could. Who would I reminisce with when she was gone? There wasn't anyone else left alive who had these memories. I would be holding them alone. What if I forgot? Would I be able to hold onto a sense of my past without her, or would it fade away with time? I felt like I was not only about to lose her, but also my one remaining connection with my father and sister. Between us we kept them alive in some way. When she died, they would die for me all over again. The loss that was about to occur felt so enormous. I wondered if my vessel was strong enough to hold all the pain.

As I lay there anticipating what was to come, I realized the futility of my thoughts. There was no way I was going to be able to deal with the totality of this situation all at once. I couldn't come to grips with the loss while she was still here. That was too much to ask of myself. I had to stay in the moment, to appreciate every second I still had with her. There would be time later, when it was reality, to face the loss. I reminded myself of Yaakov Avinu and his inability to come to terms with the death of Yosef, for the simple reason that Yosef was not dead. He had been separated from his father but he was still alive. Yaakov, of course, didn't know this. He thought his son had died. But his soul, unlike his mind, could not be deceived. And so all his efforts to grieve amounted to naught. He remained inconsolable. I took that as a lesson for myself. I wasn't going to be able to get a head start on the grieving process. As it says, "To everything there is a season, and a time to every purpose under the heaven: ...a time to weep and a time to laugh; a time to mourn and a time to dance" (*Koheles* 3:1,4). Now was still the time to laugh and dance, even in the face of the heartache. The weeping and mourning would have to wait.

I would have to remind myself of this more than once in the days that followed. It was easy for my mind to stray into the future. And when it did, I could feel my chest constrict around the pain that lay ahead and a sense of overwhelm start to descend. Quickly, I would tell myself that she was still here, that there was still life to be lived with her and that I didn't need to fast-forward. That day would arrive soon enough, and I would have more than enough time then to deal with everything. Oddly enough, I had said those same words, "She's still here," when I was just four years old, in a context not that different from the one I was in now. My mother had her first bout with cancer then and was seriously ill. She had several surgeries and radiation treatment. Something had happened in the last surgery that had created a complication, and the doctors thought she was not likely to survive. Someone, I don't know who, had the idea to bring my sister and me into her room to say goodbye to her. I remember the scene like it happened yesterday.

I was brought to the side of the bed where she lay. It was the middle of the day, but the shades were drawn so the room was dark. There were other people there. My father and sister for sure and maybe someone else; I don't remember. My mother was trying to smile at me and I heard her whisper the words, "Hi darling." Meanwhile, everyone else seemed to be crying. I don't remember doing this, but I was told later that my immediate response was to say: "Why is everyone crying; she's still here." That apparently lightened the atmosphere in the room a little. And my mother went on to say what she thought then was her goodbye. I don't remember much of what she said other than that she would always love me. Mostly I remember how thin and weak her voice sounded and how strange everything seemed. But from my words I can see that even then I was trying to help myself — and everyone else — stay in the present. That time it was even more sage advice, since as it turned out she didn't die. She went on to live many more years. This time, I probably wouldn't be spared the anticipated outcome, she probably would die. Still, it made sense not to grieve now but to enjoy whatever time we had left. She was indeed "still here."

The meeting with the funeral home came and went. I knew the routine from having handled my sister's arrangements, and I had discussed her preferences with my mother before I went. It was such a huge relief to leave there having ordered her coffin and shroud, and come home to find her laughing and smiling. I went through all the details with her and only one caught us by surprise. They had asked me for the wording of the obituary that would appear in the newspaper. It's a simple announcement that includes the name of the deceased, the date and place of death and the names of the members of her family with places of residence if still alive. It also includes an address for *shivah* and often designates a place to which contributions can be sent. That last item stumped us momentarily.

When my sister Karen, *a"h*, had died so tragically years before, I had created a fund in her name called the Karen Millhauser Maged Care Fund. She had been an extraordinary middle-school teacher, who had helped so many troubled children who otherwise would have fallen between the cracks.

When she died we received letters from hundreds of current and former students, who wrote so emotionally of the difference she had made in their lives: how she had taught them to hold their heads high; how she had made learning fun and accessible in ways that nobody had before; and how much they would miss her and her big, beautiful smile that had lit up the halls. I decided right then to create a fund for the school where she had taught for so many years, so that the students who would never know her would still be able to partake in some way of her goodness. The fund was unique in that the children themselves could go to it for help, in the same way they would have gone to her. And though she wouldn't be there to support them, at least there would be resources to help them get what they needed — whether it was counseling or tutoring or money for a school trip or an instrument or anything else they might need to ease their way. Teachers who had known my sister well sat on the board of directors and were available to receive the children's requests and to respond in ways that my sister would have wanted to, had she been there.

By now, the fund had been in existence for some time. There were fewer people at the school who still knew my sister. Some of the teachers who served on the fund's board had retired, and the principal who had been there for most of her tenure had left. When my mother died, there would be no immediate family member in the States to interface with and oversee the fund. We decided that it was time to move it to a larger organization where we could be assured that it would exist in perpetuity and wouldn't be subject to the vagaries of changing personnel. When I drafted the original fund documents, I had included a provision that would allow us to move it elsewhere. So I knew that my first step was to notify the school of our intention so that the necessary steps could be taken to close it out there. At the same time, I had to begin my search for a new home, one that would keep the fund intact as the Karen Millhauser Maged Care Fund and still use it for the benefit of children, to whom she had been so devoted.

I decided to send an e-mail to several large Jewish organizations explaining the situation and asking them if they were interested. The most enthusiastic response came from Hadassah Hospital, which has a special unit for children in need. I explained my mother's situation to them and that we would need to act fast. They were happy to work with us and within a few weeks we were able to complete the transfer. For my mother it was enormously gratifying to know that the fund that had been created in memory of her beloved daughter now had a permanent home in Israel. Hadassah sent her a beautiful large certificate with stained glass artwork commemorating the contribution. And, a plaque with the names of all of our family members was to be placed on the wall of the children's unit in Jerusalem. The whole arrangement brought her great peace and satisfaction. There was a sense of completion, of closure. She was thrilled with the idea that in her death she would be helping the Karen Millhauser Maged Care Fund to carry on its good work in its new venue. We had no question now about where to ask people to send contributions in her memory when the time came.

Had we not thought about the content of the obituary, we probably would not have thought about the fund, let alone go through all the work to move it to a new home. With everything else we were dealing with, it simply wouldn't have made it onto our radar screen. Yet, the process of doing it, not to mention the end result, turned out to be one of the enjoyable projects of this time. We discussed the various decisions that had to be made, we became acquainted with new people, and we had a sense of purpose, of doing something important that needed to be done. All of that was a blessing for my mother who, instead of being consumed by her circumstances, had something constructive and meaningful to focus on. It felt like a gift from my sister.

In the middle of all this I had a birthday. Birthdays had always been a big thing in our family. We got each other gifts and cards and generally made a fuss over the person whose birthday it was. What would be this year? I dreaded the day. How could I celebrate what I knew would be my last birthday with my mother? It felt unbearably sad. And what could we do? My mother no longer had the stamina to go anywhere. The pain was getting worse. She had lost a lot of weight and was quite fragile. I wanted to skip the whole thing. But she wouldn't hear of it. Unbeknownst to me, she had talked to my dear friend Diane, the person who was closest to us through this whole ordeal, and asked her to bring over a cake and a few other things. And she ordered a spectacular flower arrangement to be delivered on the day.

My friends started calling early on the day of my birthday, figuring that it wouldn't be easy for me. My mother didn't say all that much about it, other than to give me the usual good wishes. I realized later that it was hard for her that she had to depend on someone else to make the celebration. She was so used to doing things herself, when and how she liked to do them. This new circumstance of having to depend on and wait for someone else was not at all to her liking. As it turned out, Diane had a little emergency of her own that day and didn't get over to the house with all the birthday trappings until much later than she and my mother had planned. As the hours went by, my mother tried to hide her disappointment that we still hadn't celebrated properly. But she was never very good at disguising such feelings so I could feel that something was wrong; I just didn't know what it was. For my part, I didn't realize what she had planned and, as it wasn't at all unusual for Diane to be late, I didn't think anything of it. Finally, my mother gave up and changed into her robe to get ready for bed. She seemed so sad.

I was downstairs in the kitchen when the doorbell rang and Diane bounded in with balloons, a big birthday cake, drinks, and some presents. The atmosphere in the house was instantly transformed. My mother brightened immediately. All the disappointment that had built up in the hours before vanished. Her relief was palpable. My birthday was going to be celebrated properly after all. I could feel how deeply it mattered to her and I just wanted to cry. Here she was, possibly weeks or even days away from death, and the thing that was most important to her was celebrating my birthday. She so badly wanted to give me what she had been able to give in earlier years and had been depending on Diane to be her agent. When it looked like Diane wasn't going to come, she had been reminded of her very real limitations, of all that she could no longer do by herself, of all that she couldn't give even when she wanted to, of how dependent she was on others. It made her feel powerless and helpless in a way she had managed to avoid when she had been healthy and I had managed to shield her from in this first month of her illness by being so instantly responsive to, often even anticipating, her needs.

But she rallied quickly when the celebration got underway. We all understood the bittersweet nature of the moment, but as with Chanukah, nobody spelled it out. Instead, I opened my gifts and cut the cake like I would have any other year. Only the taking of photographs had a greater sense of urgency than in the past. Diane took many more pictures of my mother and me than she would have under normal circumstances, and my mother seemed to want to take more of Diane and me. It was as if we were all desperately trying to hold on to this last precious birthday party together through photography.

More than anything, though, we cherished the sweetness and coziness of our little gathering. We were upstairs in the den that had once been my sister's bedroom. As walking up and down the stairs became more difficult, my mother spent more and more time in this room. Somehow we never tired of it. It had a wallpaper mural on one wall that made it seem like we were by the water's edge in a little fishing village. The carpet and window treatments were brightly colored and the furniture mostly white. It was cheery and comfortable, with soft but good light. And by now it was filled with lots of plants, flowers, and cards that my mother's friends were sending almost daily.

My mother sat in the same easy chair that my father had used in his last days many years before. It had been reupholstered but looked just as it had then, which I'm sure was a source of great comfort to my mother. She had remained as devoted to him after his death as she had been when he was alive. She seemed so built for marriage and companionship that it was hard to imagine that she would flourish on her own. But she did, and remained unequivocal in her stance that she had been blessed to be married to her true soul mate.

That Diane was joining us in our celebration felt right, too. Diane was like a sister to me. We had met through Abby, her sister and my very close friend. From the first moment we saw each other, we felt a deep sense of knowing. There was something very familiar and easy in our connection. Since then, we had been by each other's sides through a lot. She was trained as an osteopath and also involved in healing. We spoke the same language, verbally and non-verbally. Diane had done a lot of osteopathic work on my mother as well. And my mother felt a deep similarity in our touch, our energy, our essences really. It was one of those remarkable things — a huge blessing of friendship so strong and so real that it penetrates all boundaries. The warmth and love among the three of us was really the greatest birthday gift of all. I was filled with gratitude.

Diane's intimate involvement with us during this time not only was a source of pleasure, it also was a source of great comfort. While I was the sole caretaker and had assumed full responsibility for my mother's care, knowing that Diane lived ten minutes away and could help in case of emergency enhanced my confidence tremendously. She was a medical professional and sure-footed in that realm. Between her and her sister Abby, who also was well-versed in the world of physical needs, I felt backed up and supported in a way that gave me great strength. Their mother had died years before, so they knew firsthand what I was going through. And independent of me, they had each developed a very loving and real relationship with my mother, so they were experiencing their own sense of sadness and loss in anticipation of what was to come.

So, while in one sense I was alone, in another I was not. We had the support and concern of many people — my mother's friends and my own — who cared about us and what was happening. Yet, during those long nights, when I lay awake in the bed beside my mother's, or dealt with whatever needed attention, I felt the solitude. As much as others cared, they were not invested in what was transpiring like I was. My one remaining family member was on her way out of this world and I was serving as her escort. It was up to me to come to terms with what was happening, to feel and deal with the myriad emotions that swirled around inside of me. I had to rise to the occasion, to muster up whatever strength, solidity, and serenity would be required to navigate through this unfamiliar territory.

One thing I knew with certainty. I was where Hashem wanted me to be, doing what He wanted me to do. My doubts about whether to be in Baltimore had been squarely resolved and my task made clear to me. That was a relief. Under normal circumstances, we are always challenged with the question of whether, in any given moment, we're doing what Hashem wants us to be doing. Even if we feel like we know generally, it's always hard to translate that generality into the specifics of everyday life. But here there was no question. My mother was dying and Hashem was asking me to take care of her, to do whatever needed to be done for her in her last days. That knowledge, in and of itself, was a source of great peace.

Because I felt so clear about my purpose at that time, it would always take me by surprise when well-meaning people would urge me to hire someone to take care of my mother so that I could "get on with my life" or "not put my life on hold." I thought their comments were bizarre. Didn't they realize that this was my life at that moment, that I was in the midst of living out a very precious chapter of my life, that I had no more interest in skipping this part of my life than I had in skipping any other. The notion that caring for my mother was something separate and unrelated to my life, that my life somehow needed to "go on," made no sense to me. I was "going on." This experience was growing me and my relationship with my mother and with Hashem in powerful ways. What else was life about if not about loving, growing, and coming closer to G-d? It seemed to me that these people were missing the point.

Even my mother at times didn't seem to get that there was

nothing I would rather have been doing. She would say that she felt bad about taking me away from my life, or interfering with my life, or somehow getting in my way. The thing she had most wanted to avoid was "being a burden." That had been her theme song all her life and the root of her staunchly independent stance. Now she feared that she was becoming what she most dreaded. Yet for me, she was the opposite of a burden. I would try to explain to her that I didn't have an agenda for my life separate from what Hashem put on my plate.

I was committed to living a spiritual life, a conscious life, a life that brought me ever closer to HaKadosh Baruch Hu. I knew that any and every circumstance could serve these ends. The key was how I chose to interact with those circumstances, my willingness to learn, to develop, to reach for new heights in myself and in my relationships with others and with Hashem. I genuinely felt myself blessed to have been given the chance to accompany my mother through this final chapter of her life, to share with her all the challenges that approaching death brings, to learn from her and give myself to her in the process. It was all a gift. Why would I want to give it away to someone else? It was growing both of us in ways nothing else could. I could feel that already.

Chapter Six

A few days later, we had our first visit from hospice. They sent someone to tell us about their services and help us with the paperwork necessary to sign up. The woman who came had that sort of cheeriness that I remembered from the nurses in the intensive care unit. These people who work on the front lines of disease and death on a daily basis seem to cultivate an attitude of optimism that many in more promising settings lack. Or, at least, they try hard to project that sense, so that they and the people they're helping don't drown in the very difficult and often distressing circumstances they find themselves in. It's infectious after a while and distracts everyone from the gravity of the situation.

For hospice, this is a very intentional posture. The whole philosophy of hospice, as their brochures proclaim, is "to ensure that each patient's remaining time is as peaceful, comfortable, and pain-free as possible"; "to promote quality of life and relationships during a very difficult time"; "to encourage patients to remain independent and in control of their lives by participating in decisions about their care." Essentially, hospice tries to help people focus on living while they are dying. It makes the disease process secondary to the person and all that he or she is about. Their personnel are all well-schooled in this philosophy and impart it along with whatever service they're providing, from paperwork assistance, to nursing care, counseling or practical help.

So the woman who came made a point of chatting with my mother and getting to know something about her and her life. My mother, always happy to get acquainted with someone new, was equally interested in hearing about this hospice worker's life and quickly turned the conversation in that direction. That was to be a pattern that would continue with all the various hospice personnel who came to the house in the months that followed. They would usually end up talking to my mother about themselves and their lives.

The nurse, who came on a twice-weekly basis, told me at the end that she had felt my mother's concern for her so strongly that she opened up more than she ever had to anyone before. She had felt such kindness from her and sensed such wisdom that she truly believed my mother to be one of G-d's angels, an ancient soul who cared so deeply about others that they were drawn to speak to her about themselves even when they knew that they were ostensibly there to take care of her. She said that everyone at hospice who had contact with her felt the same way.

I knew this ability of my mother to draw people out. It was, in large part, a function of her genuine interest in them. She allowed herself to become absorbed in what the other person was saying, to enter fully into their reality. And then she would engage in conversation about it with them as though she was intimately involved, which, for that time, she would actually feel herself to be. It was a capacity she had to leave herself and go where the other person was for whatever time she was conversing with them. They, in turn, would feel her presence with them very strongly and be inspired to share even more. She didn't do it so much with me. That was always a little perplexing since I was a person she actually was intimately involved with. But I think either it was her way of maintaining a boundary and giving me room to chart my own course, or it was her protection from knowing too much about a life that mattered to her deeply but over which she had no control. With other people, she apparently didn't feel so constrained.

Her relations with the hospice staff were no different from her relations with other people all of her life. It was obvious to me that, like most people, she was choosing to die as she had lived. In her case, that meant with dignity, courage, compassion for others — and a lid on the past firmly in place. She wasn't the least bit interested in talking about her own life, though others tried valiantly to entice her. She had decided long ago to close the door on pain and suffering, of which she had had more than her share. Her German accent, which was still strong, was an invitation for questions, but she was always able to deflect them and turn the conversation back to the other person. Even I knew very little and much of what I did know came from research and exploration I undertook on my own.

My parents were both German Jewish Holocaust refugees, who made it out just in time, but who were unable to save their parents and, in my father's case, a younger sister. They hastily said goodbye to their parents at the end of 1938, fully planning to meet again. The few letters that I was able to dig up make that very clear.

Forced into one room of their family home by Nazi soldiers, my grandparents write reassuring letters that everything is okay and they are looking forward to being reunited with the children in America and Palestine. The same when they are forced to leave even the one room and find another small flat to live in. And the same again when they are transported to a holding camp in Gurs and, as my grandfather writes, the men and women are separated. Still they try to reassure, to encourage, and to look forward to the day when everyone will be together again.

That day never came. The letters stopped. That was that. No bodies. No funerals. No graves. No closure, as we would say today. Just silence. Later, there were Red Cross tracing papers to connect a name and a place — Auschwitz, Buchenwald, Riga. And it was over. Nothing left except the formidable task of moving ahead with grief and guilt so profound that they defied words. My parents met the silence that signaled the extermination of their beloved parents and little sister with a silence of their own. They not only didn't speak about the Holocaust, but they said almost nothing about their parents and sister. There were no photographs displayed, no stories shared, and questions, when we dared to ask them, were met with "that was the past and this is the present; we live in the present."

Certainly, on the continuum of atrocities my parents are considered among the fortunate. Yet, viewed outside the lens of those extraordinary times, the picture looks different. Imagine meeting someone whose parent had been murdered and the body never recovered. We would ache for him and assume that this event weighed heavy in his life. Now imagine that both of his parents were murdered, along with his little sister, and the bodies were never recovered. We would be overwhelmed by the

90

horror this person has had to bear. Now imagine that this person married another person, who was carrying the same load. And add to the equation that each felt that he or she had an obligation to save the family members who had been lost. And that he or she had failed. And finally, throw in a wrenching and irreversible separation from homeland just as adult life is beginning. Everything that seemed certain is overthrown. Nothing is as it appeared to be while growing up.

These are wounded people. However nobly they may have carried on, they carried within them unrelenting pain and probably a host of other emotions. For my parents, and particularly my mother, I think those emotions were too great to even engage. They closed down around them and consciously or unconsciously decided to build a life on top of them. And they succeeded, as did many others, remarkably well. But there was a price.

In a sense, my mother used her pain as a springboard to reach out to others. Nobody knew or even could have guessed how much she had gone through herself. That was for her to know and nobody else. She preferred to listen and be there for other people, while keeping her own counsel. She preferred to be cheery and optimistic, without letting on in any way when she was hurting. She preferred to stay strong and resilient by not dwelling in dark and difficult places. That was her response to her life experience. That was the way she chose to cope. That was the way that worked for her. Knowing all this, and observing it for a lifetime, I wasn't surprised at her interactions with the hospice workers.

The remarkable thing was her ability to return to herself, to never lose track of her own reality even as she ventured so far into others'. Her sense of self was strong and solid. It never seemed to waiver. In my early years, this had been a source of great frustration for me, as I tried valiantly to change her, to get her to see things as I did, and to be who I wanted her to be. But she wouldn't budge. She knew who she was, she knew what was important to her, and she knew how she wanted to live her life. Her certainty in these areas in some ways challenged me to find my own place, the place where I could stand in a solidity that matched hers. My efforts in this regard took me in many directions over the years, during which time she remained a constant.

She wanted to live in the present and not speak about the past, she wanted to close off life's sorrows and focus on its pleasures, she wanted to stay in the light and not probe into darkness. She tried valiantly to impart this stance to me. But it didn't take. I could inhabit her happy haven for a while, but it never seemed real or substantial enough to sustain me. Even as a child, I would descend into dark and powerful places inside myself. "Snap out of it" she would tell me, not appreciating that this option wasn't available. She couldn't understand that. Her own will was so strong that there was no place in her experience where it couldn't take her. I was her daughter. How was it possible that my will could not do the same? She was baffled and clueless how to engage with me. She couldn't begin to imagine where I went on those dark descents, so far away were they from her own range of experience. Or maybe she just couldn't bear to. Maybe, instead of being so far away, the territory I was being drawn into was entirely too close for comfort. Maybe she couldn't risk coming too near for fear of being drawn in. Whatever the reason, she kept her distance.

So, the trajectories of our lives took us in opposite directions — though we never let go of one another. I matched her mastery of light with my own mastery of darkness, of extracting light from darkness. All the suffering, hurt, and disappointments that she excised, I examined in minute detail and tried to find in them something redeeming. It was as if, in some unspoken way, this aspect of life had been delegated to me. It took a different sort of strength and perseverance. We were both strong and both determined. We simply set our minds to different tasks. The difference, it seemed, was that hers gave her seemingly solid ground to stand on and to live life from. I, on the other hand, was always moving in the early years of my adult life. I would set out in one direction and then another in search of the solidity that she seemed to possess almost effortlessly. Her steadfastness was a constant in my ever-changing world. I rested in it occasionally, but I could never stay for long. There was something hollow and unreal about it for me. For a long time, I couldn't believe that it didn't feel that way to her, too. I would challenge her on contenting herself with such an existence, on not probing beneath the surface, on relying on platitudes.

Her reality was as unfathomable to me as mine was to her. And usually, I kept the same distance. Her reality felt sanitized and artificial to me. It didn't sustain me as it seemed to sustain her. I had to find my own center, even if it contradicted hers. Yet somehow, we were able to hold tight to each other across that great divide. She watched me search, dig, turn the soil, explore down different roads. She watched me intentionally set out to excavate the very past she had refused to discuss. I retraced her and my father's steps in Germany. I tracked down anyone still alive who knew them and their families in the distant past. I collected photographs and stories of my ancestors that had been missing from our home. When I shared them with her, she said little, though she did follow up with visits of her own to some of the people I had unearthed. Somehow, she would listen to whatever I came up with in my various explorations and then artfully find a way to move beyond and reset the status quo for herself to where it had been before.

As time went on, that actually became a strange sort of comfort. Whatever I discovered in my endless search for a deeper level of truth on which to stand, I knew that a part of my world would remain unchanged. That was a source of frustration to be sure. I wanted her to join me in my reality, or at least in recognizing the limits of hers. Yet, if that couldn't happen, and I couldn't fully join her, the next best thing seemed to be that at least I had a familiar place to visit. I couldn't have articulated any of this consciously at the time. But looking back, it seems to me that was what was going on.

During this time of her illness, long after I had come to accept and even appreciate that she was who she was, I asked her from where she drew her strength in this regard. For by now, I could only marvel at her sure-footedness, that had carried her gracefully through so many life changes and was continuing to carry her now as she approached her death. At first she wasn't sure how to answer, and she just said that this was the way G-d made her. But as she thought more about it, she offered that her Judaism and the Jewish way of life was probably the source. From there she had learned to take things as they come with thanks, praise, and prayers to G-d. She never lost track of the fact that she was a Jew and that she had a very particular place in this world because of it. Undoubtedly, her experiences as a child in Germany and as a refugee whose parents were exterminated simply because they were Jews contributed to the solidity of her Jewish identity.

I realized as I listened to her that, although I was now more Torah observant than she was, I didn't have as strong an inborn sense of myself as a Jew. My identity had been diluted in the American melting pot in which I had been raised. Even the anti-Semitism that had been rampant in my childhood didn't impress upon me my unique place as a Jew. I remembered well the signs that said "No Jews Allowed" at the local swimming pool and skating rink. But they didn't solidify my sense of myself as a Jew or encourage me to hold more strongly to my religious/ethnic identity. I considered myself an American who happened to be Jewish and who happened to have German-Jewish parents who had escaped the Holocaust. I felt myself entitled to walk right past those signs whenever I could and do as I liked, whether or not I was Jewish.

Some of my vagueness was probably a result of the way my parents chose to deal with their Holocaust past. Their silence was a deafening backdrop to a life that seemed to exist in a vacuum. Another factor was their religious affiliation. Not long after she came to America, my mother married my father, who arrived shortly after she had. They had known each other in Germany and tentatively arranged to reconnect in America if both of them were able to make it. My mother had been raised in an observant, *shomer Shabbos* home. Her father was a deeply religious man whose dream was to go to Eretz Yisrael. My father came from a non-observant home, although his grandparents on his father's side (with whom he was close) were Torah observant. Some time after my parents married, they realized that their parents had been killed in concentration camps, that they would never see them again. They were on their own in a new country, and together they decided to lead a Conservative Jewish life.

Suspended in the thin air of the present, without access to the past or any sort of family history, it was up to me to find my bearings. As far as my Judaism, that meant trying to distill something meaningful from the Conservative synagogue services we attended, the three-day-a-week afternoon Hebrew school I went to, my bat mitzvah, our home observance of all the Jewish holidays, our weekly lighting of the Shabbos candles and reciting of Kiddush and *HaMotzi*, and my nightly recitation of the Shema that my mother taught me when I was a little girl. Somehow, it all didn't add up to much of a Jewish identity inside of me. In contrast, my mother seemed to feel herself a Jew in the very cells of her body. She grew up in an observant home with a very devout father. Jews had been ostracized to some degree from the time she was very young and, in the end, she had to flee her birthplace for the sole reason that she was a Jew — the same reason her parents were murdered. Nothing had ever let her forget her Jewishness as America had let me.

All the compromises inherent in the Conservative tradition rendered it more confusing than inspiring for me. It never spoke to me and, in fact, propelled me elsewhere in search of truth. Only through G-d's grace had I found my way back to Torah, back to Judaism, and on to the *chareidi* life that I live today, where I have the sense of solidity that eluded me in my mother's world. In one short generation, the kind of cellular connection to Judaism that my mother took for granted had been totally undermined. I had to reconstruct it, which meant it would never be as organic a part of me as it was for my mother. This was an incredible reality for me to contemplate. It was only during these days of caring for my mother that I even became aware of how central her Judaism was to her sense of self. Because she wasn't Torah-observant, I had assumed it didn't play such a central role. As I talked to her, though, I realized I was wrong. That in some ways she was more solid in her Jewish identity than I was. And I felt humbled.

The Holocaust hadn't succeeded in destroying the Jews, but

it had definitely damaged the chain of transmission. Links that had held strongly for generations were weakened. I realized that becoming Torah-observant wasn't just about my own spiritual life, but about reconnecting and strengthening a link in a chain that had almost been broken. It was sobering to realize how little time it took to break something so strong and long-lasting. At the same time, I trusted that something very important was taking place in this movement away from and back again. I, and all the others like me, who had strayed from our Jewish roots only to return, were bringing back something valuable. I wasn't sure that I could articulate exactly what it was, but I knew instinctively that our wandering and our hard work to find our way back was not in vain.

I didn't hold my mother and her generation responsible for the breach. In fact, I admired her ability to hold on to as much as she had in the face of all that she had endured and all that life in America asked of immigrants in those days. Even the stories I've heard since, about the people who were able to maintain Orthodox Torah observance under those circumstances, don't diminish my respect. For my mother, where she was holding and with the questions she had, the level of *Yiddishkeit* that she was able to maintain was still an accomplishment from which I benefitted. At least I knew in my mind, if not the cells of my body, that I was a Jew. I had some background and experience in Hebrew, prayer, and the holidays. That was more than a lot of young people in my generation had. Many people's parents totally assimilated; their children knew nothing about their Jewish identity. When I wanted to come back, I didn't have to start from scratch. I already had a foundation to build on.

I also had that European connection. While my parents didn't speak of their German past, their strong accents and their distinctly European ways of doing things brought me in contact with a world that was very different from the America of my youth. I couldn't put my finger on the difference when I was a child and, as all children do, I longed for my parents to be more like my friends' American parents. My parents, too, had made up their minds to be American. They didn't speak German to us when we were children so that we wouldn't be different when we started school. It was all part of their effort to put Germany, and all that had happened there, behind them.

But when all was said and done, there were things about them that were simply not typically American. There was a certain depth, substance, dignity, and pride that had Europe written all over it. There was also a strictness, discipline, precision, formality, and punctuality that carried the imprint of Germany. And their Judaism, even if less observant than in my mother's childhood home, still seemed tethered to the tradition that was so deeply rooted in the Europe of the previous century. It still had that feeling of timelessness, of something ancient and precious. We used the *leichter* and menorah that had been in my mother's family for generations. My mother still had the *machzorim* and *siddurim* she had used as a child in Germany. The Hebrew and German on their yellowed pages spoke of a different world, a different time from modern America.

Even without words, the past found a way to creep in and, as in the other scenarios, it was up to me to find a way to make sense of it, to integrate it with the present, and to incorporate it into my own reality. That process seemed to be continuing even now, as I watched my mother graciously interact with everyone she came into contact with, even as she herself was dying. I realized that her immense capacity in this regard came from many sources. She had identified her G-d–given character traits and her Judaism, but I saw that her European upbringing and her life experiences also played a big part.

One such experience of which she spoke more openly during this time was that of being a young refugee on her own in a new country. She remembered those days as a crash course in interacting with people. She met all types — from those who were looking to take advantage, to those who genuinely wanted to be of help or befriend her. She very quickly had to learn to discriminate, to protect herself from exploitation, to connect to a wide variety of people and to form friendships from scratch. She also had to learn the ways of America, to try to understand a culture that was foreign to her, and to become proficient in a language that she hardly knew. Through all of this, she had only herself to rely on, only she could gauge what was good for her among the myriad of possibilities. It was clear that circumstances had forced her to take responsibility for herself and her choices early on in her life. They had also impressed upon her the importance of being able to relate to people. Through her challenges as a refugee, among other things, she had learned valuable lessons that had sustained her for a lifetime.

She had also garnered important insights into life from her parents. The advice they imparted to her as a child and as she set out on her own for America, stayed with her. The little she told me during this time painted a picture of a young woman who desperately didn't want to leave her parents behind in Hitler's Germany. She stayed with them until the last possible moment and held tight to their parting words. Living out her life in alignment with what they told her seemed to be her way of honoring them, as well as a source of her own strength. As I listened to the bits of the past she was now willing to share, I finally began to understand how some of the pieces of her life fit together, how she had become the woman who for so long had been an enigma to me.

Chapter Seven

By now we were into the next calendar year, and my father's *yahrtzeit* was coming up. The date fell neatly within the life-expectancy parameters the doctor had so unceremoniously offered to my mother along with her diagnosis. Ever the romantic, my mother thought that maybe she would go on the same day. That idea actually gave her some peace. It would make her exit relatively quick — six weeks or so from the day of the diagnosis — and connect her on yet another level with my father. There was something very neat and orderly about it that appealed to her. From my standpoint, it was still way too soon. I was still scrambling to adjust to a reality that she seemed to be taking in stride. But if it was her time, I, too, liked the idea that my parents would share the same *yahrtzeit*.

The *yahrtzeit* began *leil Shabbos*. We lit the *yahrtzeit* candle and then the Shabbos candles. The little den, where by now we were having all our meals and spending most of our time, shone with light. I told my mother that, in addition to giving *tzedakah* and saying Kaddish, it was customary to study Mishnah as a source of merit for the soul of the departed. An allusion to this custom is found in the letters of the Hebrew word משנה, Mishnah, which — as Arizal and Sh'lah point out — can be rearranged to form the word נשמה, *neshamah*, or soul. Although any section of the six orders of Mishnah may be studied for this purpose, there is a widespread tradition to learn chapter 7 of tractate *Mikvaos* because the initial letters of its final four *mishnayos* spell the word נשמה, *neshamah (The Complete ArtScroll Siddur, Nusach Sefard*, p. 850, according to R' Yitzchak Isaac of Komarna). My mother was more than happy to do anything that would be a source of merit for my father's soul, and she listened attentively while I read the Mishnayos to her from the siddur.

I had been reciting this chapter of Mishnah on the *yahrtzeits* of my father and sister during the years I lived in Jerusalem. It was moving for me to now be doing it in Baltimore, in the house where I grew up, with my mother who herself was close to death. I was bringing her full circle back to many of the more Orthodox observances which hadn't been a part of her adult life. Even though she didn't understand everything I was reading, she could feel the *kedushah*, the holiness, in the words and the practice. The room had an air of reverence that was palpable to both of us.

When we finished, it was time to recite the prayer that typically follows such studies. I knew this prayer always touched me deeply. I wondered how it was going to affect my mother. I read aloud:

Please, O Hashem, full of mercy, for in Your hand is the soul of all the living and the spirit of every human being, may You find favor in our Torah study and prayer for the soul of Eliyahu ben Avraham, and do with it according to Your great kindness, to open for it the gates of mercy and kindness and the gates of the Garden of Eden. Accept it with love and affection and send it Your holy and pure angels to lead it and to settle it under the Tree of Life near the souls of the righteous and devout men and women, to enjoy the radiance of Your Presence, to satiate it from Your good that is concealed for the righteous. May the body repose in the grave with proper contentment, pleasure, gladness, and peace, as it is written: "Let him enter in peace, let them rest on their beds — everyone who has lived in his proper way." And it is written: "Let the devout exult in glory, let them sing joyously upon their beds." And it is written: "If you lay down, you will not fear; when you lay down, your sleep will be sweet." And protect him from the tribulations of the grave and from worms and maggots. Forgive and pardon him for all his sins, for there is no man who is so wholly righteous on earth that he does good and never sins. Remember for him the merits and righteous deeds that he performed, and cause a spiritual flow from his soul to keep his bones fresh in the grave from the abundant good that is concealed for the righteous, as it is written: "How abundant is Your goodness that You have concealed for Your reverent ones," and it is written: "He guards all his bones, even one of them was not broken." May it rest secure, alone, and serene, from fear of evil and may it not see the threshold of Gehinnom. May his soul be bound in the Bond of Life. And may it be brought back to life with the Resuscitation of the Dead with all the dead of Your people Israel, with mercy. Amen.

"Amen," my mother said softly. She sat quietly, deep in thought. I didn't want to interrupt her reverie. I could only imagine how it felt to hear those words on the eve of one's own death. Even arranging for the coffin and burial didn't give the grave reality like this prayer did. And it made the need for Hashem's protection on the other side, for His mercy as the soul continues its journey in the next world, very real. What was my mother thinking about? Was she reflecting on her own life and where she was headed, or was she connecting with my father's *neshamah* which, in that moment, we had been trying to help. I chose to honor her privacy and she chose not to share where she had been. By the time she spoke, she had moved on. We went ahead and made Kiddush and began the Friday-night meal.

My mother was a little surprised to awaken the next morning feeling no different than she had the day before. It looked like she wasn't going to die on my father's *yahrtzeit*, after all. I could tell she was a little disappointed, so I let her know that it was fine by me that she was still here. She had to chuckle. And to concede once again that *"dehr mensch tracht un Gaut lacht* (man thinks and G-d laughs)."

These questions, of when to respect my mother's silence and when to draw her out, or even just name what was happening, were ongoing for me. I wanted to participate in this experience with her as fully as she was willing to let me. At the same time, I didn't want to invade or intrude into places in which she didn't want me to go. Because by nature my mother was such a private person and shared so little of her own inner world, it took some cajoling to get her to open up. Yet when she did, she seemed happy to have done so. Part of the problem was that by nature she was not as introspective as I was. Some of my questions would take her by surprise. "I don't know" she would say, "I never thought about that." Then a day or two later she would sometimes come back to me and say, "I thought about what you asked me," and go on to tell me whatever she had come up with. If it was a question she wasn't interested in answering, she just wouldn't get back to me on it. Then I had to decide if I wanted to try again or leave it alone.

I was very aware of the short amount of time left in which to ask my mother anything. After a lifetime of almost taking for granted that she was there, time was now running out. Anything I didn't talk about with her now would be left unsaid between us. At the same time, I didn't want these days to be weighed down with heavy conversation. A lot of the pleasure we were having with each other was in lighter moments — reminiscing, sorting through things in the house, looking at photographs, and just chatting.

For years my mother had talked about cleaning out the house, getting rid of lots of things that had been there for decades. Like many people, she had good intentions to take care of that chore herself and not leave it for me. There were all kinds of books, papers, jewelry, shoes, clothing, and other assorted objects that needed going through. In her room alone there were closets and dressers that contained things from forty or fifty years ago. We decided to tackle a few of those drawers together and soon found ourselves transported to another era, when ladies wore gloves, carried handkerchiefs, and covered their hair with kerchiefs that have long disappeared from the scene. It was an era of a certain elegance that suited my mother. We were like a couple of girls playing dress-up as we both donned elbow-length gloves and old costume jewelry. My mother remembered aloud where she had worn these things many long years ago. And it was like we were there.

We were having so much fun. It was hard to remember that she was dying. We seemed to have settled into a routine, a new way of life, and it felt like it would go on indefinitely. Friends continued to ply her with beautiful flower arrangements. The upstairs den where we spent most of our time was green and blooming. We loved watching the plants blossom, feeling their vitality feed ours. There was so much love in that room that visitors who came to see her went away energized and enlivened. People couldn't get over it. They would come to the house with some trepidation, knowing they were visiting a dear friend who was terminally ill. Their awkwardness, their fears about what to say, even their sadness, would be washed away when they saw my mother dressed and put-together as always, sitting in her favorite yellow chair, reaching out to them with the same smile and dancing eyes they had come to love. She put everyone at ease. She reassured them that she was ready to go when called, that she had lived a long and full life, that everyone has to go sometime. And she continued to show interest in all of them, in whatever was going on their lives at the moment. Nothing was too small or insignificant. She was still there with them in their trials and tribulations.

This matter of getting dressed and fixing herself up every day was no small thing. I marveled at her willingness to invest the time and energy. I often thought that had it been me, I would have opted to stay in bed some days, especially when the pain was really bad. But she had never been one to lollygag in bed. And she had never lounged around the house in bedclothes. She always got dressed in the morning in something neat and presentable and she didn't want to do anything different now. As the days went on and she grew weaker, it became harder for her to dress herself. I became her wardrobe manager, picking out her clothes with her and helping her to put them on. We decided that there was no longer any point in saving anything for a special occasion. She might as well wear the nice things that she had. If not now, when? We did the same with jewelry. We took all the special pieces — most of them gifts from my father — out of their hiding places around the house and we both wore them. It was time to enjoy all that she had.

Getting dressed made a big difference. So did making the bed. With all the medications, the restricted diet, and medical emergencies, this wasn't going to be a sick house. It was a house where there was still a lot of living and loving and learning happening. Every day was different. Some days the pain was better and other days it was worse. Some days the liquids went down easily and others there was more choking. We had to be inventive, creative, and do whatever we could to tackle the different challenges. The biggest one of all was working with the medications. Because my mother was highly sensitive to any kind of medicine, she tried to avoid it whenever she could. When her blood pressure soared after my sister's death, she tried various blood pressure medications for a few weeks, only to suffer horrendous side effects from all of them. Taking matters into her own hands, she started doing biofeedback and getting Zero Balancing treatments and managed to bring her pressure down without pills. But now she had no choice. The pain from the tumors and from nerve pressure was too great. She needed medicine badly.

The Duragesic patch which the emergency-room nurse had introduced us to was still working well for her, though we had to up the dosage along the way. But that only addressed one aspect of her pain. She needed something else along with it. That meant we were going to have try other pain medications, a prospect that frightened both of us. The problem was, that in order to find out if a particular medicine would work and if she could tolerate it, she would have to take it. Once she took it, she was susceptible to the array of terrible side effects listed in the package insert which, by the time one got through reading them, seemed worse than whatever ache or pain the medication was intended to help. We talked over the options with the hospice nurse. Nothing sounded great but we had to try something. Each prescription the nurse gave us filled us with trepidation. My mother would take the medicine and then we would wait to see what was going to happen.

One night, when we were trying yet another prescription, her eyes rolled back in her head and she went limp in my arms as I tried to help her into the bathroom. She was out and I had no idea what was happening. I remembered the instructions from hospice to call them and not 911 in case of emergency. Shaking, I dialed the hospice number and asked the operator who answered to get hold of the on-duty nurse immediately. Within a minute I got a call back and the nurse on the line talked me through what to do. She told me she would be there within the half hour and not to try to move her by myself. Together, we got her back to her bed and back to consciousness. She seemed disoriented and didn't remember what had happened. While she rested, I talked to the nurse about other possibilities for pain management and she had a good idea which the day nurse hadn't thought of. It turned out to be the answer to the pain problem for the next period of time. It was remarkable. For the second time, an emergency was the vehicle for getting us the right pain medication. I had to thank Hashem for this gift in disguise.

Within a few hours, my mother was sitting up in bed chatting on the phone with a friend. I was so relieved. When she had collapsed in my arms, I was sure she was dying. Listening to her now talking on the phone was, for me, like witnessing a resurrection. The whole episode was a good gauge for me, as the emergency nurse pointed out when she sensed my fear and distress. "She *is* dying," she told me. "There's nothing to be afraid of. The body knows how to do this." She reminded me that I had to get myself prepared, that one of these days an episode like this could well be the end, that there would be no revival. I guess she could see that I was still holding on.

The nurse's words reverberated in my mind all that night. "The body knows how to do this." I hadn't been thinking about death in quite those terms. But it was true. The process that I was witnessing was one that, since the sin of Adam and Chavah, Hashem had made part of the Creation. Death is "natural." Man is supposed to die. The body and soul are supposed to separate. The body is supposed to return to dust and the soul is supposed to go on to the next world. At some point in the future, the two are supposed to be reunited through a resurrection of the dead. Hashem programmed into us the wherewithal to do all of these things — to be born, to live, to die, and to be resurrected. Our bodies and souls know how to navigate through each of these transitions. We really don't need to be afraid.

I remembered a book I had read years before called *Gesher Hachaim: The Bridge of Life*. The author, Rabbi Tucanzinsky wrote: "Emergence from the womb constitutes corporeal birth, while detachment from the body is the birth of the soul. 'The born are to die and the dead to live' (*Avos* 4:22). One is born to die, and dies to live. 'Once a man is born, the countdown begins for him to die; once he dies the countdown to birth begins' " (*Koheles Rabbah* 7:1).

Rosa, the wonderful housekeeper who, since my sister died, came every few weeks to help my mother, said something similar to me the next day, when I told her what had happened the night before. "Ain't none of us come here to stay," she said. "We all got to walk this road sometime." I felt like Hashem was sending me messages, reminding me that what I was witnessing was nothing more or less than a part of His plan. I could relax into the rightness of it and trust that events would unfold exactly as they needed to for Him to take my mother from this world and usher her soul into the next. I could consider myself the midwife, helping her to allow her body to do what it naturally knew how to do, helping her to birth her soul.

Pain management became more complicated as the days wore on and the pain intensified. My mother was adamant that she wanted her mind to remain clear. Hospice offered her morphine repeatedly, but she always declined. She was determined to stay in control of her faculties for as long as she possibly could. So we had to keep trying different combinations of medicines and different dosages to reduce the pain. One particularly difficult day, I suggested that she try acupuncture as part of her program. Always a little uncomfortable with needles, she initially rejected the idea. I went ahead and got the name of someone good from Diane in case she changed her mind. A week later, I brought it up again and she agreed. By then, she was willing to try anything that might help, anything that might give her relief and still allow her mind to remain clear.

I called Stacey, the acupuncturist Diane had recommended, and she came to the house the next day. She and my mother hit it off instantly, as Stacey patiently explained to her how acupuncture worked and just what she would be doing. Always eager to learn and to have a new experience, my mother listened attentively and finally announced she was ready. Stacey gently inserted a few needles in different parts of her body. Having had so much energy work from me and from Diane, my mother could instantly feel her energy moving in response to the needles. To Stacey's amazement, she tracked perfectly the path that the energy was taking. By now, she was fascinated and asking lots of questions. Stacey loved it. Here was this eighty-eight year old, terminally ill woman as interested and inquisitive as the best of her acupuncture students. They agreed that she would come once a week and more if needed. By later that day, my mother sensed that the acupuncture had helped. She started to keep a little journal of the date of treatment and the effect it had on her. It was her own little experiment in the efficacy of another form of alternative medicine. If she could have found a way, she wouldn't have used anything else.

But, unfortunately, she still needed the drugs. Anything we used other than the patch had to be in liquid form, which required some coordination with the pharmacy. Doses had to be given at different intervals during the day, depending on the drug. The patch had to be changed every few days. Before long, we started using a second patch on a different place on the body, to increase the dosage and help equalize the distribution. That way one patch would be new and at the height of effectiveness, while the other was starting to wane; it helped us manage the pain better.

It was getting complicated; I could no longer keep straight in my mind what drug was administered when and when a patch needed changing. I started to keep a log, writing the date and time of each dose administered or patch changed. I also included notes if there was a bad reaction to a particular food or breakthrough pain. Keeping a record in this way was helpful on a lot of levels. It not only made it easier to administer all the medications, but it gave a sense of order, a feeling that we were starting to get a handle on this cumbersome routine. Our team, as it were, was functioning well. With G-d's help, we were meeting the challenges being presented to us daily and, strange as it may sound, taking from that a certain sense of accomplishment. We also felt ourselves working together more and more effortlessly. Some invisible barrier between us was disappearing. We were totally united in intention and purpose and taking pleasure from the flow that created.

I was also starting to hold my mother more. Touch is an integral part of me; it is also an important medium in my work. For my mother it was less so. As warm and caring as she was, her German upbringing had not educated her in the language of touch. Now she was growing more frail by the day. Always small in height and weight, she was becoming really tiny. Her bones, as I helped her bathe, protruded from her chest. I wanted to lend her the solidity and softness of my body as hers grew weaker and more angular. I would climb into her bed behind her and sit her up against my chest. My arms around her, I would encourage her to relax into me. At first it was hard for her to do. She worried that she was too heavy, that she was hurting me. When I assured her that I was fine, that she was light and comfortable for me, she let go a little bit. But she was still holding herself up. She couldn't yet relax enough to give me her full weight, to really rest into me and let me truly hold her. I felt her tension and embraced it. I appreciated how hard it was for a woman who had been holding herself up her entire lifetime to finally let go. I realized that this could well be the first time she was held with absolutely no expectation of anything in return. I had no desire but to give to her; I wasn't looking to her for anything. I only wanted her to be able to feel in the cells of her body that I was there for her, holding her, containing her, making a safe space for her.

I had worked many years to create such a space for myself. I had to learn, in the same way that I help my clients to learn, what it means to hold and contain oneself. I also had to learn how to come fully into my body, to feel myself held in the container of my own being and by G-d. My mother no longer had years to do this work herself. I wanted to transfer to her vicariously some of what I had come to know. I was patient and loving beyond any capacity I had known before. I simply sat behind her, my arms around her, breathing slowly and deeply, and I felt an enormous love, a love that truly wanted nothing but to give. I stayed there as long as it felt good to her. And then I moved away. Each day I could feel her body releasing a little more. Each day I could feel her trust of the space grow. Each day I could feel more tension drain out of her. Each day I could feel her give me a little more of her weight. Until one day, I felt her finally let go. She relaxed totally and let me hold her without any effort on her part to hold herself. My heart was so full I thought it would burst. What a gift to be able to give my mother such a complete feeling of safety, of being cared for, of being held, loved, appreciated, and respected.

My work with myself over many years had allowed me to honor her defenses — those same defenses that had so frustrated and frightened me long ago. It seemed that once I was able to embrace and honor them, she was able to let them go. I had finally made room for her just as she was, and she, in turn, made room for me. She let herself receive from me, she let me give to her from the depth of my being — something that had previously frightened her. Neither of us spoke any of this out. It was all there in the touch.

Even Rosa noticed a difference. My mother seemed to be softening and opening. Her vulnerability was shimmering beneath her strength, creating a glow around her. One day, a florist delivered a beautiful, huge flower arrangement sent to my mother by Bess, one of her oldest friends. I had run out to the grocery store for a few minutes, knowing that Rosa was there if my mother needed anything. While I was out, the flowers came. My mother saw them, read the card, and apparently burst into tears — something almost unheard of for her. Rosa, a big, warm, gentle woman herself, instinctively wrapped my tiny mother in her arms and held her as she cried. As she held her, she sang to her an old folk song she had learned as a young girl in the South.

Give me my flowers while I still live

So I can enjoy the beauty they bring.

Friends and loved ones always give you flowers when you're sick or on your dying bed.

But I'd rather have one tulip right now than a truckload of roses when I'm gone.

Please give me my flowers while I still live, so I can enjoy the beauty they bring.

Rosa just kept crooning that song, rocking her gently and letting her cry. It was a perfect response to the moment. By the time I got home, my mother was smiling inside her tears. She told me later what had happened. From her telling I could hear that the whole experience had surprised and deeply touched her. I was so grateful to Rosa for her big heart and her soulful understanding. She had given my mother a gift as beautiful as the flowers.

My mother wasn't the only one being transformed. I also was unrecognizable to myself some days. I had endless patience, boundless love, and enormous energy even when we had to be up four or five times during the night to take care of one problem or another. Usually I need a good night's sleep to function at my peak. But now it seemed that Hashem was giving me extra strength and energy, so that even a few hours of interrupted sleep was enough. I reflected on the intense love I was feeling and realized I had never known a love this pure before. I really didn't want or need anything for myself. I was so deeply gratified by giving, by enveloping her in my affection. And that it was my mother engendering these feelings in me was also startling. Though our love and commitment to each other never wavered, we hadn't always had the easiest relationship. Our strong wills had come up against each other more than once. Yet somehow, all of the years of struggle had gotten us to this point where we were able — maybe for the first time — to really see and appreciate each other in our own right. I knew this woman from a deep place inside her and inside myself. I had worked long and hard to understand her over the course of my life. When we talked about it, she joked that I probably knew her better than she knew herself. I had certainly given the subject more thought. And now I was reaping the fruits of that lifetime of labor. I was freed up and able to access this deep well of love for her that knew no bounds. The blessing was mine.

Chapter Eight

With all of the sweetness and love that we were experiencing, there was still the reality of this very eviscerating disease. My mother was growing steadily weaker. Each day, it seemed, she was confronted with the loss of some capacity that only the day before she had still taken for granted. It was hard. And it was exactly what she hadn't wanted to go through on the way to death. As the days wore on, her mental and emotional stamina were challenged in ways they had never been before. Her fierce will, her ability to move herself to a good place in virtually any circumstance, was being tested.

The more she deteriorated physically, the harder it was to access those powerful resources inside herself that had stood her in such good stead all of her life. At first she didn't want to admit to herself that her way of coping that had worked for her for a lifetime was not serving her as well now. But then she had a string of bad days when she couldn't pull herself together and get on top of the difficult feelings that were starting to plague her. And she didn't understand why.

At night, before she went to sleep, she would apologize for "not being herself" that day. I would tell her that she never had to apologize to me for being in a hard place or grappling with difficult feelings. I wanted her to feel comfortable being with whatever was going on inside of her and, given what she was going through, how could some of that not be dark and painful? I joked with her, telling her to remember that I was the one who was at home in the darkness, so she certainly didn't have to apologize to me for going there herself. And I offered to be there with her if she wanted, to listen, to hold her, to think and feel into it with her, to do whatever would be helpful for her. I reminded her that the way out of a hard place like the one she was in was to go through it, that I could be there with her, that all the strength and resources she had devoted to her old ways of coping could be harnessed in service of new ways that, at least in this circumstance, might even serve her better.

For a few nights she just listened to what I said without responding. I could see that she was having a very hard time and I felt deeply for her. I didn't know if my words were reaching her or what exactly she was trying to do. Finally, she spoke to me from her place of pain. She didn't know what was wrong with her, she felt like she wasn't herself the past few days, she couldn't understand why all of sudden she saw everything through such a dark lens when just a few days before she was fine and carrying on as she always had. She was perplexed and troubled by her state of mind but couldn't seem to do anything about it. And that bothered her tremendously.

I asked her if she was willing for me to explore it with her. I told her that if she was feeling the way she was, she could trust that something real was happening inside of her that needed attention. If we could hear and listen to the part of her that was hurting, the part of her that was at the root of these difficult feelings, she would no longer be stuck there. We could address whatever concerns were fueling her mood and tend to that vulnerable part of her that wanted her attention so badly that it literally had to stop her in her tracks, prevent her from using her old coping mechanisms.

Again she listened without saying much. Then she asked me whether I was sure that if we went into whatever it was that was bothering her we would really be able to get to a different place. She reminded me that she had never done that. That hadn't been her way of operating. I reassured her that I had walked this road many times before, that I felt sure-footed here, that Hashem would be helping us, and that I had never seen an effort to address a vulnerability go unrewarded. She might not feel a major shift right away, but she would feel some movement, some sense of change in the status quo which had bogged her down for days now. And from that little step would come the next one and the next one and the next one, until she would walk herself out of the darkness and back into the light that she so cherished.

I explained to her that some of that light that she loved so much was actually buried in the darkness, that it was our job to retrieve those sparks, that they could only be manifested in the world if people like us were willing to go in after them, to do what it took to transform them from darkness to light. This was all part of our soul work in this lifetime. I reminded her again that all of her strengths and assets that she had used so well to keep these kinds of feelings at bay, would serve her in this endeavor too. Her patience, her perseverance, her

117

intelligence, her sense of humor, her compassion, her curiosity, and her other amazing gifts would all be utilized. She had what it took to do this, no question about it.

Eventually, some of my confidence rubbed off on her and we started in. I basically asked her questions and helped her to draw out the answers from the hurting places inside herself. Apparently, the doctor's words that she had from a few days to a few months left to live had deeply penetrated her. She had taken as a given that this period, however agonizing, would be short. But a few months had already gone by and she was still very much here. The reality that she might be in this incapacitated state for an extended period of time, much like my father had to endure, was unbearable for her. She so badly wanted to go if she could no longer live life fully. She so badly didn't want to linger in pain and misery, to become a burden to me. She so badly didn't want to be increasingly dependent.

Yet obviously the timing, just how long she would be in this transition place, was up to G-d, not to her. She was afraid that if it was too prolonged she wouldn't be able to manage it in the way she wanted to. She didn't know how long she could sustain her good cheer, how long she could will herself to get up and get dressed every day when it took every ounce of her energy, how long she could tolerate the pain and the horrid array of medications she was taking to control it, how long she could endure the liquid diet and the reality that she would never eat real food again. Looked at through the lens of a long haul, so much of what she was going through and, until now, had managed so nobly seemed overwhelming, at least in her mind.

And on top of all that, she felt bad that she wasn't grateful to still be here, given the wondrous time that we were having. She appreciated what I was doing and what was happening between us so much, yet it was starting to be overshadowed by all the demands the illness was placing on her physically, emotionally, and mentally. And she didn't want that to happen. But she was starting to feel powerless to control where her feelings were taking her. In a way, she was feeling things in spite of herself and didn't know what to do about it. Her old ways of getting past strong emotions just weren't working. And she felt terrible about that. She wanted to be acting differently than she had the last few days but couldn't seem to do it. She didn't want to be down or irritated or impatient or frustrated or in any of the other emotional states that threatened her usual good spirits and measured way of being. She wanted to be the way she had always been. It had served her in all sorts of trying circumstances before. She couldn't understand why, this time, she wasn't quite able to get there.

Listening to her bear her heart only increased my love for her. Here was a woman who for a lifetime had tried to live on top of her vulnerability, who had been able to will herself to do anything she needed to do or go anyplace she needed to go inside herself to stay above the pain and heartache of life. This iron-clad capacity was what had allowed her to say "Snap out of it" to me when I was a child and honestly believe that she was helping me to develop in a way that would serve me in the long term.

And now, for the first time in her life, she hadn't been able to snap out of it herself. She was willing to admit that and to open the next door that needed to be opened inside of her in order to move forward. Plenty of people in that circumstance would have chosen to stay miserable. They might have suffered in silence or complained bitterly, but they wouldn't have chosen, at that stage of life, to open a new frontier in themselves. But my mother had the courage at that moment to embrace change, to walk down a road with me that she had assiduously avoided until then, to trust me to guide and support her in the process, and to venture into unknown territory without any sense of where it would take her.

Just saying out the different things that were going through her mind and heart lightened her load considerably. Her occasional tears lifted another part of the burden, and my complete understanding and validation of all that she was saying yet another. Together, we explored both the outer reality that she now found herself in and the inner reality that was governing her response to it. We talked a lot about the expectations she had of herself and where they came from. We looked at how those expectations could be shifted to allow her to embrace her present reality more comfortably and give herself more room to simply be human. We talked about her fear of dependence and of being a burden and where those feelings were hooked up inside of her. We looked at what it would take for her to absorb that I wasn't experiencing her or our situation in that way, that I was truly grateful for the opportunity to share this chapter of her life with her, that circumstances that she labeled as burdensome were not so for me, but rather were a treasured opportunity.

And we talked a lot about the soul. I explained to her, as I had before, that death occurs when the soul has completed its work in this world, that as long as she was here there was more for her soul to do or to learn, that even the struggle she was finding herself in now was part of that learning and growth — part of her soul's work. Nothing that happened fell outside that paradigm. She was doing important work, no matter how she was feeling. We talked about the conflict that she felt raging inside of her between the part of her that was ready to go and the part of her that was still tethered to this world. She could feel the tension between the two, but didn't seem able to come down on one side or the other. Feeling them both simultaneously confused her.

Again, I was able to understand deeply what she was saying and to appreciate the challenge she was facing. I talked to her about holding the tension of opposites, of these two pulls inside herself. Using her breath, I helped her to experiment with a way of staying with both of them comfortably and trusting that in its right time, the conflict would resolve itself. She didn't need to do anything to make that happen. She just needed to be able to stay with the reality of what was, the reality that part of her was ready to go and part of her wanted to stay. She let me know that I was a big part of the pull that held her here, that made it hard for her to leave. I understood and appreciated that without her saying it but found it helpful when she did. I was going through my own evolving process of coming to terms with her departure. I wanted to be there for her and, at the same time, not hold her back. So I, too, was feeling the tension, the pull in different directions, and told her so. Even though we didn't go any further in our discussion, at least we had named something that was obviously weighing heavy on both of us.

By the time we were finished, it was late and time for her to go to sleep. When I went to give her a kiss goodnight as I always did, she took my hand, looked at me, and said, "Thank you, darling. I feel so different, so much better, like a different person again. I don't know how to thank you enough. You really saved me."

"You saved yourself," I told her. "You were the one who was willing to open up, to let me in, to be honest with yourself, and to go into places that you used to work so hard to stay out of. It was awesome to witness," I said, "and a privilege to be a part of."

She smiled a sort of dreamy smile at me and turned over to go to sleep. I could see that she felt so good about herself, so happy to have taken the risk to go where she did and with me. I, too, felt wonderful. I felt the pleasure of having been able to be there for her, of being able to help her. And I felt the joy of having shared with her on yet a deeper level, of seeing her and having her see me in ways that we hadn't experienced before. What was happening was so real, so rich, so exciting, and so meaningful. I thanked Hashem with all my heart and got ready for bed myself.

The next day, my mother awoke in some ways feeling stronger emotionally than she had since the beginning of the whole ordeal. Instead of seeing this time only as dying time and using it to prepare herself for death, she began viewing it as an important chapter of her life, to be lived as fully as possible. She started to shift her focus from how long it would be to what she could be doing. We talked about it a lot over the next days and weeks. It was in the context of those discussions that the idea of this book — at that point to be written in two voices — came into being.

We felt like we were both learning and growing so much by virtue of this experience that we were having together. The more we talked about it, the more we saw an opportunity to help other people who were or would be facing similar challenges. My mother was energized by the idea of writing a book together. We brainstormed about the framework, the major ideas we wanted to cover, the vignettes that we wanted to include and how to go about getting started. At that point, we had tackled a lot of the physical problems presented by the illness and had settled down into a routine of sorts.

On the food front, I encouraged my mother to supplement

her liquid diet, which by this time was horribly monotonous, with regular food. It took a lot of convincing, but I finally persuaded her that most of the pleasure of eating — the flavor and texture — comes with the biting into and chewing of food. Swallowing and digesting are really secondary in that regard. I had the idea that I could prepare her favorite dishes, she could take the food into her mouth, chew it, swallow whatever part of it totally liquefied, and spit out the rest. The very idea of such a thing was appalling to her initially. She was so proper in her ways that spitting out anything didn't seem like an option. But the more I talked about it with her, the more willing she became to give it a try.

Even though she was always small and thin, she enjoyed food. And the illness had snatched away her ability to eat almost overnight. She didn't even have a chance to savor the last bite of anything she loved. She went from having swallowing difficulties that she had every reason to believe were nothing more than a symptom of acid reflux, to finding out that she had an esophageal tumor that was not operable, that she was dying, and that she would never eat real food again as long as she lived.

In the face of the death sentence she had received, not being able to eat solid foods didn't register that high on her Richter scale. But as time went on, the loss became more real. Why suffer that loss on top of everything else, I thought to myself. Why not have the fun of eating all the things she liked and just not swallow them? Although at first she wouldn't hear of it, after a time, I talked her into trying it once. I made portabella mushrooms and onions, a dish that she enjoyed. Armed with lots of napkins into which she could discreetly spit out whatever couldn't be reduced to liquid, we had our meal together.

It was such an enormous pleasure for her to eat again, to have the variety of tastes and textures she had been missing during the months of her liquid-only diet. She realized that she could dispose of the part she couldn't swallow quite neatly and that not only was I not bothered by it, I was thrilled to share with her the joy of eating once again. That also meant she could have challah on Shabbos, another thing she had dearly missed. And the chicken and meat in her soups no longer had to be reduced to flavorings, but could be chewed on as well. It opened up culinary worlds and gave her back a piece of what she had lost. It was a great innovation.

At the other end of food intake, was the matter of elimination. With a limited diet, little movement, and a lot of medications that constipate, it's hard for someone who is seriously ill to maintain regularity. It's a well-known challenge to hospice workers, who come armed with all sorts of theories and remedies. This was an area where we already had had one bad episode that had landed us in the emergency room. We were not anxious for a repeat performance. We learned from experience that no matter what anyone said, it was up to us to know her body, what was reasonable for her in terms of frequency, how her body responded to the various products, and in what combination and how often to use them. Too many times, we listened to what this or that nurse or doctor said, only to find ourselves with difficulties that could have been avoided if we followed our own instincts. We also discovered that acupuncture was helpful in this area, as were Diane's osteopathic interventions.

The recognition that we were on our own in terms of navigating through these challenges dawned on us slowly. At the beginning we liked to think that there were experts to whom we could pose these types of questions and from whom we would get answers that worked. Over time, we realized that a lot of the answers we were getting were generic; they didn't take her into account in any specific or very personal way. By this point we really knew the ins and outs of how her body was operating better than all the professionals. After all, we were the ones living with the reality twenty-four hours a day. So we started to take more responsibility for figuring out solutions to even these very practical problems. We would listen to whatever the nurse recommended, factor in what we knew both about my mother's system specifically and about other possible ways to deal with whatever the problem was, and then we would decide what to try.

This approach helped us in many ways. We stopped feeling let down by people who advised us to do things that didn't work. We grew more confident in our own abilities to handle various problems that arose. We learned to experiment with different approaches until we found something that worked. We were less worried when something that had worked for a period of time stopped working or became less effective, because we trusted our ability to come up with something new. And when we succeeded, for example, in healing a bedsore with vitamin E instead of the various creams hospice gave us which didn't work, we felt great. We even shared our innovation with the hospice nurse who was happy to learn about it and passed it on to other patients. Though different from the challenges each of us had been meeting in daily life before the illness, these were among the challenges of this period, and it was no less satisfying to meet them with Hashem's help.

Our appreciation of the things we were learning and accomplishing in these often difficult circumstances strengthened both of us. We didn't measure ourselves or our days by what we had been doing before all this happened.

Rather, we accepted that this was our reality now and looked at how to live that reality as fully and joyfully as possible. The importance of this shift can't be overstated. It's tempting to look at life — especially life that's been compromised by illness — through a lens that is built on comparisons to what once was or what might have been. While it usually is necessary to grieve the loss of various capacities, abilities, and opportunities, at some point it is essential to move beyond the past and into the reality of the present, with all its limitations and changes.

For while awareness of, and relationship to, the past are essential, it is only in the present that life can be fully lived. Each moment, no matter what it is, presents its own unique window of experience. By coming fully into that moment, we're able to partake of the particular experience it offers. And we can trust that it is precisely that experience that the soul needs in order to grow and develop in the way Hashem intended. If our attention is focused on what used to be or could have been, we miss the possibilities inherent in the present. Instead, we see only what is lost or lacking, and we can easily become despondent or embittered. For the most part, my mother somehow had the fortitude not to do that. She didn't dwell on what she could no longer do but instead on what she could still do. It reminded me of an article that Diane had shown me about the violinist Yitzhak Perlman.

He was giving a recital at New York's Lincoln Center. A victim of childhood polio, he came on stage as he always did, walking slowly and painfully, with leg braces and crutches. Once seated, he laboriously lay down the crutches and removed the braces. Only then was he ready to begin playing. At the beginning of the orchestral work in which he was the featured soloist, he broke a string. Everyone heard it snap. The orchestra stopped playing, expecting him to make his way back off stage to replace the string. Everyone assumed there would be a delay. Instead, Perlman did something unthinkable. He stayed where he was, with the imperfect instrument, and nodded to the conductor to restart the piece.

A reporter for the Houston Chronicle, who was in the audience, later wrote:

> And he played with such passion and such power and such purity as they had never heard before. Of course, anyone knows that it is impossible to play a symphonic work with just three strings. I know that, and you know that, but that night Yitzhak Perlman refused to know that... When he finished, there was an awesome silence in the room. And then people rose and cheered. There was an extraordinary outburst of applause from every corner of the auditorium. We were all on our feet, screaming and cheering, doing everything we could to show how much we appreciated what he had done.
>
> Then Perlman said something to the audience as unforgettable as his performance. He said, "You know, sometimes it is the artist's task to find out how much music you can still make with what you have left."

With terminal cancer, what is left changes from week to week and day to day. By now, my mother had great difficulty walking on her own. But she could still make her way from the bedroom or den to the bathroom by holding on to furniture or the walls along the way. And for that she was grateful. She so treasured her ability to move on her own steam. She also could no longer get in or out of the bathtub on her own but, with my help, was still able to take warm baths, as she had for so much of her life. We just had to keep coming up with ingenious ways to get her out, as she grew weaker and less able to assist. But we managed and she continued to enjoy her baths right up until the end. And when her birthday came, we celebrated as we had mine, with everything we had. I even got her a new outfit so she could once more have the pleasure of wearing something new.

As I helped my mother with more and more everyday tasks, we were both poignantly aware of the role reversal that was taking place, and it touched our hearts deeply. Life was coming full circle. I was now tending to her in many of the same ways she had tended to me. One moment in particular struck both of us. I had just washed her hair and was combing it out, trying not to yank on the tangles. As she sat there and I stood behind her, we were both transported back decades to mornings in that same bathroom when I was a little girl. I used to sit just where she now sat and she used to stand just where I now stood, combing out my wet hair. There was something about being in the exact same physical space that drove home to both of us the cycle of life. It's an awareness that eludes most of us in the prime of our lives, this recognition that some day, G-d-willing, we too will grow old and be on the receiving end of loving ministrations.

We remembered aloud together, somewhat nostalgic for that earlier time when there was so much yet ahead for both of us. At the same time, we appreciated all that had transpired since then, all that G-d had given to both of us in the interim. And then we returned to the present, once more connecting ourselves to the preciousness of the moment and all that this chapter of life had to offer.

Chapter Nine

At the same time as we were doing all we could with what was left, my mother and I were continuing to talk about and explore the subject of death. We read books that talked about the soul, the World to Come, other dimensions of existence, and the inevitable transition that each of us makes from this world to the next. She was interested and fascinated by the Torah perspective and only sorry that she hadn't delved into this realm of study before. She felt like there was so much for her to learn and now so little time.

This approach of being open and forthcoming about death, of talking and reading about it, was right for my mother, the result of an array of experiences and beliefs. She felt that her life, with all its ups and downs, had been full and long; a certain sense of peace and well-being about her life had come to her years earlier after my sister, *z"l*, died; her husband, *z"l*, who she felt was her true soulmate, had preceded her in death by many years; she accepted without question or reservation Hashem's will for her; she trusted that He had a plan, that everything was *bashert* — including the moment of one's death; she was not afraid of death; and she believed in an afterlife, in the eternity of the soul. In earlier years she had talked freely of her preferences were she to become incapacitated, and she had executed a health-care power-of-attorney, detailing those preferences. Death was not a subject she shied away from even before this recent illncss. Her ease made it that much easier for me and I'm sure, in part, inspired my own.

For I, too, was comfortable in this realm. An early childhood experience, described in my book *Inner Torah: Where Consciousness and Kedushah Meet*, had given me access to a dimension beyond the physical. I understood in the very cells of my body that this world is not all there is. I knew with a deep certainty that the soul continues on beyond this lifetime. Many years earlier, together with my mother, I had taken care of my father through his terminal illness, by which time I had already lost a close friend in a freak accident. With my father, I had the powerful experience of being alone with him when he seemed to have died and then, miraculously, came back and described to me the light he had seen and the choice he had been given. This occurred about two months before his actual death. I also took care of my sister in her last days. And in my healing practice, I had ministered to a number of women facing death from cancer.

From my own spiritual experiences and from these powerful encounters with others as they confronted death, I knew firsthand the opportunity it offers the soul. As sad as is the separation from loved ones, there comes a time when the soul is more drawn to the next world than it is to this one and it begins the process of taking leave. The chance to witness and be a part of this transition is every bit as awesome and transformative as witnessing and being part of a birth, even though at the same time, it is deeply painful. So I, too, like my mother, was not afraid. I, too, had total trust in Hashem. For us, given who we both were and our level of comfort in this realm, talking about death was not a problem.

For someone else it very well might be. Everyone is different. Everyone's *neshamah* has different needs and navigates through the world in different ways. I was well aware that my mother's approach to her last days might not work for someone else. I knew from my own experience that her approach to other aspects of life that she had valiantly tried to impart hadn't worked for me. I was grateful that, at least when it came to death, we were on the same page. Some of her friends told her that they could never do what she was doing, that they wouldn't want to know so clearly what was happening, that they would want to attempt treatment even if they knew it was unlikely to work, just to stave off the inevitable. And some of my friends said the same about what I was doing, that they couldn't do it, that it would be too painful and sad, that they would be too scared and uncomfortable.

Around this time I also read an article in *Yated Ne'eman* entitled "Denial vs. Reality" that reinforced my awareness of people's differences in this realm. Written by Rav Nochum Eisenstein of Lakewood, New Jersey, the article looked at the question of whether it's proper for a doctor or relative to inform a seriously ill person that his death is imminent or to volunteer an estimate of how long the person has to live (as my mother's doctor had done). Rav Eisenstein wrote:

> It is a *zechus* for a person to say *viduy*, to confess his aveiros, before his death. The halachah requires those present when a person is about to expire to encourage him

to say *viduy*. This requirement, however, is limited to a person near death, a state known as 'goses.' Because a realization of his pending death can cause depression and quicken his demise (Yoreh Deah 338), a deathly ill person should not necessarily be informed of the severity of his condition. A competent Rav should in each case be consulted for exact direction in this most serious matter.

The article goes on to discuss the author's experience with his own father who, he learned, had only a few days to live. He asked one of his *rebbeim* whether he should inform his father of his condition and have him say *viduy*, or not. According to the article,

The *rebbi* advised as follows: Your father is elderly and sick in the hospital. He is getting no stronger and, quite to the contrary, grows weaker by the day. Certainly, that realization is crossing his mind and he is saying *viduy.*

The *rebbi* further related that when the *gaon* Rav Shlomo Heiman, *zt"l*, was ill and went to the Mayo clinic for a diagnosis in the early 1940's, he received the verdict that he had six months to live. Rav Heiman commented that at that moment they destroyed his life. For the next six months, until his *petirah*, he was barely able to function. Prior to the diagnosis, although in constant pain, he managed to function; after he was apprised of the prognosis he could not. The thought of his demise was overpowering. The obvious point is that it is reasonable to assume that the idea of his death certainly had crossed his mind. So what distressed him so much more after he learned the actual state of affairs?

There is a concept of *liba l'pumya lo galya* — the heart does not disclose to the mouth. Human psychology allows for denial; and as long as the issue hovers just under the surface it can be denied. When it comes out into the open, however, reality must be faced. Rav Heiman certainly entertained the idea of his demise, but, being human, he was able to submerge it. When the idea transformed from a possibility to a reality, however, he could no longer deny it, and that powerful notion overtook him....

My mother had invoked the power of denial at many other junctures in her life. It was one of our big bones of contention over the years. There were things that I wanted her to face that she resolutely refused to look at head-on. And there were things that she wanted me to keep submerged beneath the surface that I insisted on bringing squarely to light, where they would be undeniable. It had taken each of us years to appreciate and even learn from each other's strategies, to understand, as Rav Eisenstein concluded his article, "There is a time and place for sheltering, and a time and place for revealing the truth." Fortunately for us, this was a time when we both were committed to knowing and talking about the truth.

Still, there was one subject that we didn't talk about so freely. That was the matter of our separation, that we were headed toward the moment when we would never again see or talk to each other in this world. It was the one topic that would instantly bring tears to my mother's eyes. It was made even more difficult for her by the fact that I would be without anyone from my family of origin once she was gone. These were hard things for her to look at. We had touched on them very briefly the night we talked about what was bothering her. But for the most part, we talked around them. We thought aloud about my eventual return to Israel, about selling or renting her house, about things that would inevitably happen on the other side of her departure. But we didn't talk about how sad and painful this final separation was for both of us. It seemed we were tacitly agreeing to postpone this conversation which I, at least, wanted very much to have.

I got my first sense of this when, some time after the diagnosis, I asked her to talk to me on tape. I wanted to be able to hear her voice after she was gone. She was most reluctant to do it, partly out of a certain shyness and self-consciousness, and partly probably out of this place where she did want to use denial. But I persevered and eventually convinced her to do it. She wanted me to ask her questions so that she didn't have to think of what to talk about it. I could see that she was afraid that it would be too emotional for her, this making of a tape of words to her daughter as she prepared to depart this world. It felt too much like saying goodbye, something she had never liked to do. The question-answer format put it more in the realm of an interview, which felt easier to handle. So that's what we did. It felt a little contrived as we were doing it, but I was still happy at the thought of having a record of her voice.

The sound of her voice was part of my cells. It had surrounded me from the time I was in the womb. As a child she read and sang to me constantly. Speech, more than touch, was her primary medium for connecting with me. So accustomed was I to her voice that I didn't even hear her heavy German accent. Her cadence was simply what was familiar to me. Only when I would hear others ask her where she was from was I reminded that she had an accent.

So we, too, had our places of sheltering amidst the truth we were doing our best to take in. And sometimes it would surprise us both when reality broke through. It happened most vividly before Pesach. I had started to ready the house shortly after Purim. My mother was worried that on top of everything else, it would be too much work for me to prepare for Pesach. But Hashem gave me the extra strength I needed and I dove into cleaning, buying and *toiveling* new dishes and utensils, ordering matzah, and planning the menu for Seder night. We remembered that the year before we had spent Pesach in the intensive care unit. Compared to where we were now, that seemed good. At least then she had been on the mend. Now she was on her way out. Yet, when we were in intensive care, we had remembered where we were a little more than a year earlier — on safari in Zimbabwe — and felt ourselves in bad straits. Clearly, it was all relative.

We just don't know what Hashem has in store for us. No matter how bad we think something is, it definitely helps to remind ourselves that it could always be worse. I remember one day when I was taking care of my sister. She was feeling particularly bad that day and said aloud, more to herself than to me, "It can't get worse than this." I felt a sinking feeling inside of me when I heard her words, and I quickly said, "Don't say that. Of course it can get worse, G-d forbid." She immediately realized the folly of her statement and said, "You're right, I take it back." I never forgot that exchange because it did get worse, much worse — a few weeks later she was dead, something neither of us, in our wildest imaginations, would have expected to happen.

These kinds of experiences have made it easy for me to count my blessings every day, to be grateful for every minute that I'm well and able-bodied, and to appreciate simply being alive no matter what is going on. I've been through enough ups and downs in my life to know that as long as I'm still here and as long as there is a semblance of movement in my inner world, even the most difficult terrain can be traversed with Hashem's help. That is a source of enormous comfort and strength for me, and I try to impart it to the women with whom I work, for I see the same thing happening in their lives. I am blessed to be able to witness the incredible capacity of so many women to deal with enormous challenges. It's inspiring and humbling at the same time.

One of those women actually inspired my mother. She was a woman I had worked with in Jerusalem after she was diagnosed with breast cancer that had already metastasized to the bones. She had married only a year before she became ill, and she was now fighting for her life. Yet remarkably, she was full of optimism, love, good humor, and an amazing reservoir of spiritual inspiration. She called the house to talk to me while I was taking care of my mother. My mother answered the phone and the two of them chatted for a few minutes. I don't know what was said, but I know that my mother got off the phone feeling enlivened and enriched. She couldn't get over it. Here was this young woman on death's doorstep, who never even had a chance to have a family of her own, so full of life that she could communicate energy and exuberance on the phone to someone she had never met.

I appreciated that my mother could recognize and receive this woman's special gifts. It seemed that her awareness of the qualities of the people around her was heightened during this time. In her encounters with her friends and mine, she seemed uniquely able to assess where people were and what was happening with them. It was almost as though some veil was slowly being lifted. She was being given access to a dimension of truth that is usually hidden. I had that sense very strongly one day when we were talking and I mentioned that never having had children was the one aspect of my life that was still sometimes hard for me. She was quiet for a moment and I wasn't quite sure where she was or what she was thinking. She seemed to be looking off in the distance, somewhere beyond where I could see. Then she said very quietly and directly, "You better get over that. G-d has other plans for you."

That was it. One sentence. But delivered with such conviction and clarity that it stopped me in my tracks. Knowing she wasn't one to commiserate for long, I hadn't expected her to get deep into my emotional reality. Still, I was surprised that she had only one sentence to utter in response to my heartfelt revelation. Apparently, from where she sat, there was nothing else to say. She had seen and stated a truth and that was that. Her words penetrated me deeply. From the moment I heard them, they resonated as real inside me for reasons that I couldn't explain. It was more of a felt sensation. I wanted to know more but she had no more to say. She still seemed slightly removed from the reality of the room in which we were sitting. And that one sentence continued to hang in the air. It was so unequivocal. I would recall it many times in the months and years ahead.

Her response was even more surprising because the subject was one that had affected her life as well. She had never been blessed with grandchildren. While she had never complained, I knew it wasn't an easy situation for her. We had both found ways to express our love for children and to contribute to their lives in various capacities. For me, it was also one of the realms in which I was privileged to be able to help others through Inner Torah. And my mother was close to the grandchildren of a number of her friends, as I was close to the children of a number of mine. Still, it wasn't the same as family of one's own. This was a time when she could have expressed her disappointment, as well. But she didn't. Something more compelling had called her and she had responded to that.

These kinds of flirtations with worlds beyond this one were starting to happen more and more. When I looked at her, she would seem to be somewhere else. Her eyes appeared to be looking through something, as though they were penetrating some unseen barrier and reaching into a realm not accessible in everyday life. It was in one of those moments, when I was opening the box of Pesach dishes from the year before, that my mother suddenly exclaimed in a voice laden with emotion, "This is my last Pesach, my last Seder." From the sound of her voice and the look on her face, I sensed that she must have just glimpsed a vision of her own death.

A few seconds later I knew I was right because she went on to say that she didn't want to be alone when she died, but she also didn't want me to go through a terrible experience. I figured she was thinking about the moment of my father's death, which apparently had been difficult. I had always regretted not being present during his last moments and there was absolutely no way, if I could help it, that I was going to be anywhere but by her side when she took her last breath. I let her know that she had nothing to think or worry about. I wanted to be there with her when her time came, and I wasn't the least bit worried about how difficult it might be. As far as I was concerned, nothing could be more difficult than not being there and I said so clearly enough that she seemed satisfied and relieved.

For all our talk about death, this particular exchange had a reality to it that was different from our other conversations. Her words seemed to have come from another dimension, one that carried more weight and had more power than everyday language. We were both a little stunned by the intensity of the awareness that had just passed through her and that she had expressed to me. My mother even seemed a little disoriented, and I helped her into bed to take a rest. When she awoke, the moment had passed, and we were back to our Pesach plans and preparations, with death once more in the background.

As a Torah-observant Jew, I did more to prepare for Pesach than my mother had done when I was growing up. She watched with pleasure as I took the house apart, cleaning and getting rid of *chametz* in a way that I think was more reminiscent of her own childhood. The Seder itself was something on which she had never compromised. We had always had a full, traditional Seder and read the Haggadah in its entirety. When her own family was no longer around for Pesach, my mother had joined the families of her friends who also celebrated in a traditional way. She had never missed Seder in her life and this year would be no exception. We set the table in the little den upstairs, arranged the matzah and Seder plate, and prepared to go through the Haggadah together. While I had used all sorts of interesting Haggadahs with commentaries during my years in Jerusalem, this year I opted to use the same simple yellow-and-red Manishevitz Haggadahs that had seen us through all of our family Seders. It contained only the Hebrew text with an English translation, no commentary. Yet, as it turned out, this was to be the highest, holiest Seder of my life.

It's not easy to explain what exactly happened. All I know is that by the time we got to the second part of Hallel, we both felt ourselves on another plane of existence. The words themselves, said with more fervor and devotion than I had ever known, transported us to a realm beyond time and space. I sensed what was happening to me and wondered where my mother was at that moment. Only later did I find out that she had allowed herself to be carried to the same extraordinary place. She had never had such an experience before. Neither one of us knew what had propelled us to the level we had reached. And we couldn't really talk about it, beyond acknowledging that something remarkable had happened. Words could never do it justice. We both were still basking in the light we had accessed. Without speaking, we realized that we each just wanted to stay with the experience. There was nothing to say or do but be grateful. We had been given a tremendous gift from HaKadosh Baruch Hu.

For me, there was a certain irony. After all my years in Jerusalem, and all the *sedarim* I had participated in with various rabbis and other learned people that had gone into the wee hours of the morning, with people cultivating spiritual experience through reams of commentary, the most powerful experience of all had come in the house I grew up in, with my mother, using the simple Haggadah of my youth. I realized that her proximity to death probably had a lot to do with what happened. It's said that the *Shechinah* hovers around very ill people. Also, my mother herself occasionally seemed to have been in contact with some other dimension of reality in the days leading up to the Seder. And I knew my *kavanah* that night had transcended anything I had ever known or experienced. Somehow, the combination of all these things had touched us both in a powerful way.

On the second night of Pesach I began counting the *omer* with my mother. As is explained,

> The Torah commands that from the second day of Pesach — the day the Omer offering of new barley is brought in the Temple — forty-nine days are to be counted; and the festival of Shavuot celebrated on the fiftieth day. This period is called *Sefiras HaOmer*, the Counting of the Omer. The *Sefirah* count also recalls an earlier event. During the seven weeks following the Exodus, our ancestors prepared themselves for receiving the Torah at Mount Sinai. This

140

responsibility to prepare oneself to receive the Torah is present every year, as we relive the Exodus from bondage and materialism, and strive to be worthy of the gift of Torah. In ancient times, the *Sefirah* period was a time of rejoicing, but it is now observed as a time of semi-mourning because of several reasons: the absence of the Temple; the death of Rabbi Akiva's 24,000 students during 33 days of the *Sefirah*; and a string of bloody massacres of Jewish communities during the Crusades.

(ArtScroll Siddur, *Nusach Sefard*, footnote, pp. 312–316)

This year was the first time my mother counted the *omer*. She quickly took to it and looked forward to the counting and our discussion of the particular *sefirah* for each night. There was something very powerful about counting *omer* on the road to dying. The cleansing of the soul that it is meant to accomplish has even greater importance for one approaching death. The significance of the counting, and the spiritual work it stimulated, was not lost on my mother. She knew that she was preparing to come before Hashem.

This knowledge seemed reinforced by the periods of what appeared to be sleep, that overtook my mother more and more as the days went on. I would find her sitting in her chair with her eyes closed, far away somewhere. When she opened her eyes, it seemed that she wasn't quite sure if she had been sleeping or just where she had been. It would sometimes take a moment for her to orient herself in the present. The stillness in the house was palpable when she floated off on these otherworldly journeys. At those times, I felt as though I was the guardian of sacred space, protecting her reverie from any sort of intrusion. They reminded me of the year before, when she had come to me for energy work, and had seemed to be drifting out of this world as I worked on her. I had wondered then whether she was flirting with worlds beyond our own but, at that point, didn't feel it to be an immediate concern. Now things were different. Now I could feel her *neshamah* wandering off from time to time, almost as though it was exploring the territory to which it was headed.

But things of this world still continued to beckon. The week after Pesach, I managed to find a dentist to come to the house. All the liquid medications had left an uncomfortable residue in my mother's mouth that brushing and rinsing just couldn't seem to get rid of. Anybody who's been sick for an extended period of time knows how much it means to have a clean mouth, especially for someone who is meticulous about such things. It took a lot of phone calls, but I finally found a man who had made home dental visits to the sick and elderly his life's work. He was good natured and worked easily in the unconventional settings in which he found himself. He told us that he couldn't bear to be in a dental office all day, that he much preferred to be out and about, and that he liked helping people in difficult circumstances feel better. For us, he was yet another angel. Someone who was able to do just what was needed when it was needed with genuine kindness and compassion. He teased my mother about still having all of her wisdom teeth. "You were supposed to have given your wisdom to us already," he told her. They laughed together and went on to chat about the state of the world today, when wisdom seems to be in short supply. When he finished, my mother couldn't thank him enough. She felt so much better, it was amazing.

A few days later, the weather outside was so beautiful that I couldn't bear for her to miss it. It was one of those perfect spring days, with the sun shining warm and bright. I wanted her to have the pleasure of feeling the warmth on her face, of seeing the buds on the trees, of breathing the fresh, clean air. Rosa was there that day to help straighten up the house. Together we got her downstairs, into a wheelchair I had borrowed from hospice, and out on the back patio. Every spring, around this time, Rosa and my mother would clean up the screened-in porch and ready it for use. During the winter months, the porch furniture was covered to protect it from snow and rain. By the spring there was usually a thick layer of dirt everywhere.

Rosa and I decided that we would clean the porch and my mother could watch and supervise from her perch on the patio. There was a lot of good-natured joking and kidding as we worked, but I could feel my mother's sadness at being sidelined even from such an uninviting task. Somehow, being confined to a wheelchair on this beautiful day, when any other year she would be hard at work, readying the porch where she loved to sit throughout the spring and summer, was making her reality real again in yet another way. I could feel how badly she wished it was otherwise.

Meanwhile, Rosa had started to sing, as she often did. She would usually start by kind of humming under her breath. Then she would begin to sing softly to herself. I found her sound soothing and soulful. I wanted to hear more. "Rosa," I asked her, "could you sing louder, it's so beautiful to hear." Rosa looked a little surprised when she heard my request. I realized that she probably didn't even know she was singing; it was so second-nature to her. Then, for reasons I didn't understand until she started singing aloud, she seemed a little reluctant. "Oh, I don't know," she said.

"Come on, Rosa. Whatever that was you were singing is really moving. I'd like to hear it and I'm sure Mom would too."

"Okay," she said, with a tone of voice that seemed to say 'you asked for it,' and she began:

Steal away, steal away, steal away home.

I ain't got long to stay here.

My Lord calls me.

He calls me by the thunder, he warns me by the lightning, the trumpets sound within my soul.

I ain't got long to stay here.

Steal away, steal away, steal away home.

I ain't got long to stay here.

We were all silent when she finished. There was something haunting and powerful about the song and the way she sang it. And, of course, the message wasn't lost on any of us. "That's right," my mother finally said. "The Lord calls us and we have to go. That's life." In saying those words she seemed to regain her perspective, to remind herself once again of where she was in life's journey and, for probably the hundredth or even thousandth time, to let go of her longing for things to be different.

We had talked about it several times already — this pendulum that seemed to swing inside of her between readiness for death and desire to be in life. She loved life so much and got so much joy from even the simplest things. There was definitely a part of her that wanted to go on, to keep living. If she could have, she would have bounded out of that wheelchair and right back into life, into all of her activities and friends, into helping and doing. Yet at the same time, there was another part of her that was ready to go if that was G-d's will for her. She wasn't afraid of death. She felt a certain sense of peace, of completion. What was hard for her was this place in-between, this place in which she felt suspended between life and death, moving endlessly between them. From here she couldn't fully embrace one or the other as she liked to do. Instead, she had to straddle these two opposite poles, to know them both intimately and simultaneously. She had to sit in the warm spring sunshine knowing that she had very little time left. She had to say goodbye to life, to all the people and things she had adored, over and over again as the days and weeks stretched into months.

Unwittingly, in my desire to give her the pleasure of feeling the sun on her face, I had also made her face more things that weren't and would be no more. I could see that the experience was affecting her, but I didn't know exactly how. It had been months since she had been outside. It was also the first time she had to use a wheelchair. I could sense her taking it all in, registering her reactions to both, and though she tried to put up a good front, I could tell it wasn't easy for her. The next day she declined my offer to go outside and sit on the freshly cleaned porch.

Over the next few days, it seemed that her energy picked up. But at the same time, the pain seemed to be increasing. It was getting harder for her to find a comfortable position to lie in. Stacey came and tried some different acupuncture points, and we tried a slightly different routine with the medications. Meanwhile, her spirits remained high. She wore her new birthday outfit on Shabbos and we did some great learning together. In an odd way, it felt like we were in sync with the energy of spring, that we were in a fresh place, ripe with potential. I assumed that one day soon she might want to go outside again. I even thought that I might find a way to take her to the ocean, another place she had always loved. And then, of course, there was the book that we hadn't yet started to write.

Chapter Ten

A few weeks earlier, my mother had made the comment, "I want to do what the elephants do."

"What's that, Mom?" I asked her.

"When an old elephant is ready to die, he leaves the herd, goes off by himself, lays down and dies. The whole thing is very natural, very dignified," she offered by way of explanation. Shortly after she made that comment, I came across a little blue porcelain elephant pendant she had bought in Africa. I showed it to her and told her it reminded me of what she had said. She was delighted and immediately put it on the chain she was wearing. By now that chain also held a little pink-and-white pendant that had been my sister's as a child, on which was written the beginning of the *pasuk* in *Tehillim* "If I forget thee, O Jerusalem..." For weeks now, she had worn the chain with her little elephant and Jerusalem pendants, her wedding band, and my father's ring every day. She took it off only to bathe. When visitors asked about the elephant, she

146

would tell them what she had told me.

The Sunday following our wonderful Shabbos had more activity than usual. The next-door neighbors who had just returned from a trip came to show my mother photographs. After they left, she observed that in prior years they had always brought her a little souvenir from their annual trip. She noticed that this year they hadn't, without drawing the obvious conclusion aloud. Abby came and devised an elaborate setup of pillows to help my mother lie down more comfortably. She worked hard to find a way to cushion her and support her arms and legs, trying out all sorts of permutations along the way. I took photographs of the two of them in their pile of pillows, as Abby tried, along with my mother, to feel what combination worked best. We had a good time. But for some reason, as I walked Abby out to her car, I commented that I was worried that my mother and I had not yet really said goodbye. Abby's reaction was not to worry, it seemed like there was still plenty of time. "It probably would have been too soon if you had tried to do it before," she said, and I felt somewhat reassured but still concerned.

By the time I got back into the house, my mother told me she didn't feel right. She couldn't say exactly what was wrong, just that something didn't feel right. She didn't think she had energy for the bath which we had planned for that evening. By now, taking a bath was a fairly big production, but it was worth it because it was so relaxing and pleasurable. We had to time it with the changing of the Duragesic patches, because they couldn't get wet. So if we didn't do it that night, we would have to wait some time. I encouraged her to muster whatever strength she had and take a bath. I reminded her how good it always made her feel. Particularly if she was now feeling strange, the bath might be helpful. She was worried that she wouldn't be able to help me at all, that it would be too much for me. She didn't want me to hurt my back. I assured her that it would be fine, that we would manage, not to worry. So she took off her chain with her pendants and rings, placed it carefully on the table, and we maneuvered into the bathroom.

As soon as I helped her into the tub, she was happy she had opted to go forward with our plan. The warm water was soothing and relaxing. I sat nearby, talking quietly with her. I sensed that something was going on, but I didn't know what. It felt like she was distracted somehow, somewhere else. I didn't want her to fall asleep in there so I continued to engage her, but in a gentle way that wouldn't jar her. When it came time for her to get out, she got very anxious. She didn't feel like she could do anything to help me lift her. I tried to reassure her that it would be all right, that I could do it on my own — even though I wasn't so sure myself. Once again, it felt like Hashem gave me Herculean strength to do what would otherwise have been impossible. With one movement I was able to lift her to the edge of the tub, really before either one of us even knew what was happening. It felt like a miracle.

As I reached for the towel, she said, "This was my last bath." I was so stunned that for a moment I didn't know what to say. She didn't even seem to be saying it *to* me, but rather just stating it aloud as a fact. I don't remember my exact words in response, but I think I tried to tell her that it wasn't so or she couldn't be so sure or something inane like that. I don't think I was able to absorb the full impact of what she was saying. Somehow, within the span of about an hour and a half we had gone from a seemingly normal day to something I had never seen or felt before. Something strange and unfamiliar was definitely happening. I had no idea where we were, so I just kept doing what needed to be done in the moment.

The next challenge was getting her from the bathroom to her bedroom and into bed. Usually, if I held onto her or held her up she could move her feet and we could get where we needed to go. That was how we had made it into the bathroom not that long before. But by now she didn't even have that much capacity. I had to get her there on my own which, again, Hashem helped me to do in a way that I don't even recall. She was so very tired and so grateful to be in bed. Within minutes she was asleep. But the night turned out to be a restless one. A short while later she half awoke and started saying "I can't anymore." I could tell she was somewhere between sleep and waking. I responded, "You don't have to." She repeated, "I can't anymore." And again I said, "You don't have to, you can let go, it's okay."

Moments later she was asleep again. A few hours after that she woke up and wanted me to continue reading to her from the book we had started on Shabbos. It was Rabbi David Aaron's book entitled: *SEEING GOD: Ten Life-Changing Lessons of the Kabbalah*. His discussion of the *sefirot*, the ten qualities of Hashem, seemed to speak to her in a way that other texts hadn't, or maybe she was in a different place in terms of her ability to hear and understand the words. Whatever it was, I could see that she was engrossed in the words I was reading. By now it was after 2:00 a.m. The energy in the room was powerful, holy even. It was as though we were being held in some suspended state. I just kept reading.

Eventually, she dozed off again. I put down the book and turned out the light. What exactly was happening, I wondered. She had been in such an energetic place the week before, had such a good Shabbos and day on Sunday, it was hard to believe that this was the end. Was it another downturn from which she would rally? Would she wake up in the morning like every

149

other morning in recent months and have her instant breakfast drink? Would she not wake up ever again? I had no idea. By some miracle, I managed to fall asleep for a few hours myself. When I awoke she was still sound asleep. Hours went by. No change. She just slept.

I wondered what to do about pain medication. By now she was overdue, but I hadn't wanted to disturb her. The hospice nurse came while she was sleeping and also didn't disturb her. She told me to try to get some medication into her a little later if she woke up at all. For the most part she slept, but started to half-wake every few hours. I would usually manage to get some sherbet and medication into her then. I called Diane, who was out of town that day, to tell her what was happening. She told me she would come over that night as soon as she got home, probably around 11 or 11:30 p.m. I was grateful. The house was eerily silent. I was aware of how much life-force we had generated up till then. It had not felt like a house of death, though clearly she was dying. But now it was starting to. Her essence was less palpable. Her sleep was less the sleep of rejuvenation and more the sleep of transition.

I kept vigil beside her. For the most part she seemed peaceful, but sometimes she would cry out. Concerned about bedsores, I would turn or somehow move her position every few hours. Mostly, I prayed. I so much wanted her not to suffer. When Diane came, it was easier to get some nourishment and pain meds into her. We propped her up, with Diane leaning behind her, and I was able to give her almost a full dosage. She didn't seem aware, but she was swallowing and cooperating to the extent she was able. I talked her through every little thing that I did, explaining and checking in with her constantly. I knew that somewhere in her consciousness she could hear me and would be helped by knowing exactly what we were doing even though she couldn't acknowledge it or respond.

Diane went to sleep in the little bedroom adjoining my mother's room, and I lay down on the bed next to my mother. About 4:00 a.m., I felt a wave of fear engulf me, as the reality of her leaving hit full force. I cried hard from a deep place inside myself. Diane reassured me that I had the capacity to contain myself and my mother through this transition. She reminded me that I had felt intense fear at each turn in the road on this journey and invariably it had turned into something beautiful. This was another step. Having a chance to go fully into my own feelings for a time was a blessing. Throughout it, my mother slept. I felt stronger on the other side of my tears and more ready to be with whatever lay ahead.

A short time later my mother yelled in a clear, loud voice I had never heard before, "Get off my back, let me go." The resonance in her voice was so strong yet she herself still seemed to be asleep. I held her hand and talked quietly to her, hoping to help ease whatever horror she was encountering in her mysterious travels. I wanted nothing more than to be with her, beside her, wherever she was in the process. For more than a day now, the communication had been one way. I talked to her, however far away she seemed, explaining, comforting, loving, tending. Then, early Tuesday morning she spoke to me. "Do I have a nurse here?" she asked. I answered, "No, do you want a nurse?" And then a second later I added, "I'm here." There was a silence, as though it was taking her time to digest and process what I was saying. Then she said: "You're the best."

Her words brought tears to my eyes. From far away, she was acknowledging my loving ministrations, letting me know that she had complete and utter faith in me, surrendering to my care even further as she entrusted me with her final hours. I felt

Hashem with us very strongly at that moment. It was almost as though as my mother dropped more into me, He strengthened His hold on us. Until these last days, I could feel my mother continuing to carry and hold herself even as she relied more and more on me. We were both manning the ship, though she was allowing herself to relax and receive my love and care. But in these last days, that was no longer the case. I was on my own in a different way. She would no longer be able to participate, even in the minimal ways she had until now. Nor would her spirit be present in the same way to infuse the house with light and life. She was on her way out, and with that question she had signaled me to reflect on whether I could carry alone what was to come.

Diane wasn't in the room at the time but came in a few minutes later. I let her know that my mother seemed more aware and Diane made her presence known to her, something which wouldn't have been possible the night before. My mother said, "Oh, *kinder*,' with such a soft and loving voice that we both melted. Those two words communicated so much. Diane then had to leave for a while. I walked her to the door, and when I returned to my mother's room I heard her say, "Why is everybody here?" I started to explain that only Diane had been here, and then I realized that she was looking beyond me somehow, as though her eyes were seeing through or past my body to another scene entirely.

She repeated, "Why is everybody here?" This time I knew enough not to try to answer in everyday terms. I just sat quietly and waited. Her arms stretched out in front of her and wafted up toward the ceiling for a few seconds. A minute or so later she addressed my father, z"l, as "darling," with a name and tone of voice she used only for him. Her arms again reached out and up. She seemed to talk to him briefly, and then she turned to my sister, *z"l*, and started talking to her by name. I sat perfectly still beside her, feeling myself very strongly in the presence of my father and sister. A family reunion! I could hardly believe it. I was so happy to feel them in the room with us. When I told Diane about it later, she got the chills. She could sense from my words how real the experience had been and what it had meant to me to be with them all again. I was overjoyed.

Meanwhile, my mother was continuing to engage with unseen presences. Her words started to get more anguished and suddenly turned into cries. She switched from English to German, and the next thing I heard her cry out was, "Mama, Mutti" and later, "Papa." Words poured from her mouth. I don't understand German so I didn't know what she was saying, but her pain, distress, and anguish were unmistakable. I sat motionless, in awe of what I was witnessing. Finally, on her deathbed, she was breaking the long-held silence. She was pouring out her heart to her parents, dead under such awful conditions so many years before. On the one hand, I regretted not understanding the content, and on the other, it felt fitting somehow that this part of herself that she had chosen to keep private would remain private. The conversation continued on and off over the next hour or so. There would be a time of silence followed by another spate of German, or simply the cry of "Mama" or "Papa." I was so happy for her that she was having this meeting, that she was finally able to speak so passionately and openly. I couldn't help wondering what life would have been like if she had been able to relieve herself of this load earlier. Still, I was grateful it was happening now and that I could witness it and silently support her in it. For I didn't say a word the whole time this was going on. I didn't want to interfere in the slightest. I hardly even moved a muscle. The whole thing was so awesome to behold.

By late Tuesday night I could no longer get any medication into her by mouth. She would complain about her back from time to time, but she didn't seem to have enough of a swallowing reflex to get anything down. Several times that night she tried to talk, but always in German so I couldn't understand. I could tell it frustrated her and repeatedly encouraged her to speak in English instead, but she didn't except for one time. She said, "Up, up." I sat her up, propped against me. She said again, "Up, up." I didn't know what else I could do for her. As I was thinking what it could be that she wanted, she said, "Oh, it's too up for you." I smiled to myself as I gently laid her back down. She had been trying to get somewhere higher, when she realized it was beyond where I was able to go. Wherever she was now was definitely "too up" for me.

Diane left Wednesday morning to go back to work. She drove away about nine and then came back fifteen minutes later for one more goodbye. She had a private conversation with my mother and left the room with tears in her eyes. I felt how much she loved my mother and me, how much she was with us whether or not she was physically present and I was strengthened. Abby was supposed to come later that day. She was stopping off at a Jewish bookstore on the way to get me a book on the halachah (Jewish law) on death and mourning, so I would know exactly what I had to do.

For a time during the late morning on Wednesday, my mother seemed more agitated. Periodically, she would cry out, "I can't anymore," and always I would tell her that she didn't have to, she could rest, relax, let go, do whatever she needed to do. The amazing thing was how strong, clear, and resonant her yell was. I had never heard such a powerful sound coming from my mother. In a funny sort of way, it impressed me. I decided to lay down with her, to hold her in my arms and give her whatever comfort I could. I saw that something was getting more difficult, that she was going through something more challenging. I wanted her to feel in her cells that she wasn't alone. I talked and sang to her a little bit and gently stroked her head. At one point she said quietly, "I want to go home." And I understood.

By the time Abby arrived, things were more peaceful and calm. My mother actually opened her eyes a few times. Together, Abby and I sat her up, with Abby behind her and me in front holding her hands. Abby told her how much she loved her and together we both sent love and light into her body through our hands — and she smiled the most beatific smile I've ever seen. We were so happy to be in contact with her and to feel, even if only briefly, the glow of her presence in the room. Even though she couldn't speak, it was clear that she was there with us, that we were in real communication with her. It was another treasured moment.

Unfortunately, it didn't last. The hospice nurse came a short while later, and while she was there my mother screamed out, "My back, my back." She was obviously in pain so we started talking about medication for her. As we were talking, my mother yelled in that clear, strong voice I had heard the day before, "Medicine, medicine. All I hear is medicine. I don't want any more medicine." We were all so startled, and for a moment it was hard not to laugh. That had been her stance all her life. She disliked medications immensely, reacted to them strongly, and tried to avoid them whenever she could. Here she was at the very end of her life, not really able to communicate in any regular way, and yet something in her, something at the depth of her being, had found the wherewithal to send out this strong statement. I figured it was partly in reaction to my attempts over the last few days to get medication into her. In taking care to explain what I was doing, I probably used the word medicine a lot, and now the hospice nurse was also using it. Whatever it was, it was another sign that some part of her was still very much with us.

At that point the nurse asked if she could have a few minutes alone with her to say goodbye. I knew my mother had meant a lot to her so I didn't object. This particular nurse had talked to my mother about many things. She was the one who had opened herself in ways that surprised her. I don't know what she said in the few moments she had alone with her, but when I went in after she left, my mother mentioned the nurse's name and then said "I'm tired." To the very end, my mother had been the supportive listener, using whatever energy she had to take in another's words. And now, finally, she was tired. I lay down beside her again and held her in my arms to help keep her calm. Occasionally she got agitated, more when we had to move her than any other time. But the risk of bedsores was real and we wanted to prevent them if we could. During one of the moves, she said, again in a very clear voice that seemed to emanate from far away, "You're killing me; I'm going to kill you."

Abby worried that hearing those words would upset me. But it didn't. I could feel that my mother was wrestling with forces which we couldn't perceive and mustering whatever strength she had to contend with them. I just wanted to be with her and do whatever I could to keep her comfortable and safe as she labored to leave this world. Whatever obstacles she was encountering on her way were put there by Hashem for her soul's benefit. Whatever challenges she still was having to face and overcome in this world would serve her well in the next. I just wanted to give her all the support, strength, and love I could as she went through this awesome process that we are all destined to go through. I spent most of the day laying there with her. Abby left sometime in the afternoon to work and planned to return late that night.

About 4:00 p.m. I called Stacey, the acupuncturist. I told her my mother had taken a turn for the worse since Sunday, that I thought we were now close to death. I told her that the treatment she had given my mother the previous Friday had helped her a lot with the pain and thought maybe she could help again. I told her that she wasn't alert, that she seemed to be working through different things. Stacey was happy that I had called and said she would be there as soon as she could that night.

About 6:30 p.m. I started to give my mother morphine. The hospice nurse had reviewed with me how to administer it and had left it to my discretion to decide when to start. I knew my mother's preference was not to use it. I held off as long as I could, as long as I felt it was in service of her process not to have it. By now, though, it seemed that she was in more pain and enduring needless suffering. I felt I had to make the decision for her. There was no way to ask her and get her consent. It was the first time I had to take matters in my own hands and do something counter to her expressed wishes. I was a little sorry that she didn't get to call the shots all the way through, but I felt the time had come and that I would be remiss in my duties if I didn't give it to her. So, with a somewhat heavy heart, I did. I could see her making an effort to swallow and her tongue went to where the morphine was.

A few hours later, before I could administer the second dose, my mother said in a very small but still audible voice, "Please give me the medicine." I could hardly believe my ears. It was as though she knew I felt conflicted about giving her the morphine and was letting me know that she wanted it now. She was taking responsibility for herself right to the end. It was so in keeping with how she had lived, I could only marvel.

Stacey came at about 9:00 p.m. to treat her. Meanwhile, I continued to give her morphine at the intervals the nurse had suggested. Abby came back around 11:00 p.m. and we went to turn her so that she wouldn't have constant pressure on the same spots. I stayed with her and Abby went to sleep in the next room. Periodically, my mother would say something in German, and occasionally she screamed out. I never left her side. Sometime around 3:00 a.m. I went to get Abby to help me turn her again. At this point my mother seemed very far away and unable to move a muscle on her own. Abby and I got into position to move her. Abby was on the side and behind her while I was on the side and in front. As we moved her, my arm reached across her. To my total and complete amazement, she leaned forward and kissed my right wrist on the inside. I couldn't believe it and probably still wouldn't if I hadn't immediately said aloud to Abby, "I just got kissed." I couldn't imagine how she had mustered up the strength to move her head that distance and exert the energy necessary to plant that kiss. I hadn't thought she was even conscious of what was going on or what we were doing or who was standing where or anything. And then, out of the blue, I receive the gift of her kiss. Her last kiss. The way in the end she chose to say goodbye. No words. Just a kiss.

Abby left for work around 9:00 a.m. and at 10:30 Rosa came. My mother was sleeping and peaceful at that point. I had called the hospice nurse early in the morning to find out whether I could give more morphine and at shorter intervals. My mother's screams in the night let me know she was still in quite a bit of pain. The nurse agreed and said she would be by later that day. I was happy that the nurse was coming, because I was a little concerned that the way I was administering the morphine put my mother at risk of choking. As it turned out, I was doing it just fine. It was actually the nurse who subjected her to a crisis. She tried to show me how it was no problem and giving morphine didn't need to be handled so gingerly. Sure enough, my mother started to choke. The nurse had to sit her up and turn her over to enable her to breathe again. I was horrified. I had taken such care with every little thing and here this nurse had acted hastily and cavalierly and caused a real problem.

Given how my sister had left this world and the residue of agony that I still carried from that, even the thought that professional incompetence might be involved in any way in my mother's death made me ill. It didn't matter to me that she was obviously on the verge of death anyway. Anything that interfered with her body's natural process and hastened her death in any way, no matter how slight, would be untenable for me. I was shaking. The nurse left the room to make a phone call. While she was gone my mother went into distress again, still trying to get over what had just happened. I called anxiously to the nurse and was frustrated when it took her some time to come back into the room. Rosa witnessed this whole thing and couldn't believe it.

While the hospice experience overall had been a very positive one for us, this last episode was a reminder that no matter how good the professional help, often there is no substitute for the type of care and attention provided by someone who knows and loves the patient. In our case, I don't know whether the nurse's casualness and seeming lack of concern was because she was so used to dealing with death, or because she couldn't bear to see my mother go, but whatever it was it was very disturbing. Rosa thought it was a good reminder to me that I was doing just fine on my own, probably better than a nurse would have done, because I loved my mother so much and was so devoted to her care.

After the nurse left, Rosa and I moved my mother to get her comfortable and rearranged the pillows under her head to give her more support. She did look like a little angel lying there. I continued to lay with her for a time and then, instinctively felt that I should no longer be touching her, and I moved over to the bed beside her. I sensed that she needed the space to ready herself to go and that my continuing to be in physical contact with her was no longer beneficial. It was time to begin the next level of separation. The only thing I continued to do physically was to swab her mouth with water from time to time and administer the morphine at the required intervals. Otherwise my contact with her was verbal only, talking to her, praying, and reciting Psalms.

Sitting beside her, I picked up the book Abby had gotten for me the day before, entitled *Mourning in Halachah,* and began reading the sections on death. I learned that a person in his last hours of life, i.e. in the final process of dying, is termed a *gosess* and that there are *halachos* on how to deal with a *gosess*. One is not allowed to touch a *gosess* (Rambam, *Hilchos Aveilus* 4:5). The footnote expounded on this prohibition, citing a quote from Tractate *Semachos*, "Whoever touches [the *gosess*] is shedding blood. To what may this be compared? To a sputtering candle. If someone touches it, it immediately goes out." One is also not allowed to do anything, however small and seemingly insignificant, that would hasten the death of a *gosess*.

I was very moved to see my intuitive responses so clearly

---

*   *Mourning in Halachah: The Laws and Customs of the Year of Mourning,* Rabbi Chaim Binyamin Goldberg, published by Mesorah Publications, Ltd. Excerpts reprinted with permission from the publisher.

reflected in the halachah. Halachah is spiritual law, it directs our actions according to the needs of the soul. In this situation, my soul had told me at some point to stop touching my mother. It had alerted me to the fact that my touch at this time would somehow interfere with her dying process. Likewise, my soul was clear that a careless action by the nurse that would hasten my mother's death by any amount of time, no matter how short, would be a serious problem. The hospice nurse was not Jewish. From her perspective, death was anyway imminent. It didn't seem to concern her too much if an action of hers brought it on slightly sooner. This nonchalant attitude toward time of death is rampant in the non-Jewish world, which looks to condone such things as doctor-assisted suicide and other forms of euthanasia. But Judaism knows that any interval of time a soul is in this world is significant and a matter for Hashem alone. No person can possibly fathom what work a soul is doing in its last hours, minutes, and seconds of life. And no person should dare interfere.

Chapter Eleven

*A*s anyone who has sat at the bedside of one who is dying is aware, it is truly a sacred time. The air in the room is charged with a special energy. There is a sense of vastness and of awe in the waiting for what is to come. It is an enormous privilege to be present at such a time, and even more so with one's parent. Halachah recognizes this as well. In *Mourning in Halachah*, it is written that "it is of great significance that a person's children and relatives be present when his soul departs" (*Mourning in Halachah* ch. 3, sec. 16). The footnote to that statement reads:

> See *Ma'avar Yabok* (5:27), who states: "Undoubtedly the deceased receives pleasure from the presence of his living family at the time when his soul departs, as he took pleasure in his family and friends [during his lifetime]...as is mentioned in the Zohar, Parashas Vayechi, on the verse (Genesis 46:4), *And Joseph will put his hand on your eyes*. This

[being present at his parent's death] undoubtedly is a benefit which the son does for his father, because the son serves as a chariot for the father, just as we find that the Twelve Tribes constituted a chariot for Jacob; and the same relationship exists between a Torah teacher and his students... From this we learn that if the son is present at the time of his father's death, this will be a kindness of the father towards the son and the son towards the father." *Ma'avar Yabok* further discusses this topic at length. He also discusses the Torah's account of how Abraham, Yitzchak, and Jacob were all buried by their sons. "It seems that it is a great satisfaction for the father when his sons occupy themselves with his burial. This certainly is also of great merit and benefit to the son, both during his lifetime and after his death. It is not for nought that Jewish custom places great insistence on this point..." (fn. 48).

In the same section that I read about the importance of being present at a parent's death, I read about the importance of refraining from crying when the soul departs. The explanation given is that those who cry cause the dying person suffering. "*Sefer Chassidim* cautions that those present should not cry out when the soul leaves the body; otherwise, it might return to the body and undergo severe suffering" (*Mourning in Halachah* ch. 3, sec. 16). That, too, I could feel instinctively. My sense was that during this time when my mother's soul was in the process of departing, and even more at the actual moment of departure, she would need me to support her in the direction she was heading, and not do anything that would hold her or call her back. In that regard, refraining from crying felt like another act of love, something else I could give her.

Another place where I saw my instincts confirmed by

halachah is in the requirement to stay with a person who is about to die.

> When a person is about to die, one is not allowed to leave him, so that he will not be alone when his soul departs. *Shulchan Aruch (Yoreh De'ah* 339:4). See *Shach* there. And *Be'er HaGolah* there, citing *Kol Bo*, explains that the soul becomes desolate if the dying person is alone when it leaves the body. It is a mitzvah to stand next to a person when the soul departs, as it is said (Psalms 49:10-11), *He will live eternally; he will not see the pit, for he saw the wise die. Rama (Yoreh De'ah* 339:4), citing *Hagahos Alfasi* on *Perek Elu Megalchin.*
>
> *(Mourning in Halachah,* ch. 3, sec. 12, fn. 40,41)*

Reading these words reminded me of my conversation with my mother right before Pesach when she had the vision of her impending death. She knew she didn't want to be alone and yet worried whether I should be there or not. My response to her at that time was unequivocal — there was no way, with Hashem's help, that I would be anywhere but with her when that time came. I was so clear that I wanted and needed to be there and that her allowing me to be with her would be a gift to me.

Studying these halachos as I sat beside my mother was comforting. I felt the truth and the deep wisdom of the Jewish tradition. I was grateful to be getting guidance from a source that spoke in terms of the soul's needs, that recognized the awesomeness of this time, and that was clear about what needed to be done.

One thing that I hadn't sensed before but when I read it felt exactly right involved kindling a light. I read:

> It is a Jewish custom to kindle a light during the weekdays

by the *gosess*. *See Ma'avar Yabok* (*Sefas Emes Section 15*): The Jewish custom is to kindle lights by the gosess. The reason is known. The Sages tell us that a light drives away harmful spiritual forces (mazikim), even at night, the time of their predominance... However the light should not be placed right beside his bed, but in the vicinity of the head of the bed (*Gesher HaChaim* [2:3:2]).

(*Mourning in Halachah*, ch. 3, sec. 24, fn. 59, 60)

I happened to have a beautiful large purple candle that, after reading those words, I lit and placed near the head of the bed. That too gave me comfort.

By now it was Thursday afternoon and the sky outside started to turn dark. Next thing I knew a major thunderstorm rolled in. The lightning lit up the sky and the thunder claps were loud and long. It was Rosa's song in real time. "My Lord calls me. He calls me by the thunder, he warns me by the lightning, the trumpets sound within my soul. I ain't got long to stay here." As soon as Rosa heard the thunder, she came into my mother's bedroom wide-eyed. She couldn't believe what was happening. When Rosa was a girl, she was taught to stop whatever she was doing during a thunderstorm and sit down. As Rosa explained it, "That's G-d working and we're not supposed to work." So for the next few hours, while the thunder and lightning continued, Rosa sat in the room with us. It was an unusually long thunderstorm. I couldn't quite believe it myself. Here I sat beside my dying mother, with lightning and thunder crashing all around me. The candle flame softly lit the room. I read Psalms from time to time, but mostly we sat in silence.

At that point, about 4:30 p.m., she was still trying to swallow the morphine I gave her and her tongue was still going to it in her mouth. I could only give her a few drops at a time and then would have to wait before I could give her more. It took about forty-five minutes to give her the full dosage. Rosa watched as I gently and carefully tended to her and told me she could feel all the love that went into my every move. I really appreciated her presence. She was so sensitive to the moment, so conscious of the sacred dimension of all that was happening, and so able to be a witness without imposing on the space or me in any way. It was really a blessing.

As the hours went on, I noticed longer intervals between my mother's breaths. Sometimes they seemed interminable. I started to wonder whether the next breath was even coming. But somehow it always did, and I slowly accustomed myself to this new breath pattern. It seemed that everything was slowing down. We were held in a suspended stillness interrupted by tiny ripples of life force. My prayers intensified.

I had heard the mailman come earlier in the afternoon but had not gone down to get the mail. About 7:00 p.m. I left my mother's room and went to the kitchen. The next dose of morphine was scheduled for 7:30, and I knew it could take as long as an hour to get it in. This was a good time to eat something while Rosa continued to watch my mother. I stopped first to get the mail and saw a little package in the mailbox. I opened it and found inside a big white tee-shirt with a pretty design on the front. At first I didn't know what it was. Then I remembered that one of the yogurt brands had sponsored a promotion, offering a tee-shirt in return for a certain number of lids from the yogurt containers. For years my mother had a yogurt and an apple for lunch each day, so it was easy for her to accumulate the necessary lids. Though participating in such promotions was not something she usually did, she had made up her mind to get the tee-shirt for Rosa, and so had dutifully saved the lids and sent them in. She had done all this a long time ago, well before she got sick. But somehow, the company had never gotten around to sending the tee-shirt. And now here it was.

I went back upstairs and said to Rosa, "You won't believe it. Look what just came — this tee-shirt that my mother got for you through a yogurt promotion. She saved the necessary number of lids and sent them in ages ago and it just came today, while you're here. It's amazing. It's like she's giving you one last gift before she goes." Rosa had tears in her eyes as she took the shirt from me. I could see how much it meant to her. She had gotten very close to my mother over the years they had known each other. My mother had been there for her when her husband had died not that long before and had helped her get back on her feet. And now she was preparing to say goodbye to my mother. I heard her talking softly to her as I went back downstairs, thanking her, telling her how much she loved her, how beautiful she looked. And she told her that it was all right for her to leave us and go to be with her husband and daughter, that we would be fine, that we would always be friends, that we could never forget her, that we would always love her and that she would always live in our hearts. When I came back into the room Rosa looked at me and said quietly, "She loved everybody, but she had a special love for you."

At 7:30 p.m. I started to administer the next dose of morphine. This time, my mother didn't react at all, no more swallowing reflex or tongue tasting. I finished at about 8:15 and went back to focusing on her breath. The intervals between breaths were getting even longer. Everything seemed to be slowing down even more. For some reason, it didn't dawn on me that we must be very close to the end. Instead, I found myself thinking about what would be that night when Diane came. Each stage in the process seemed to have a life of its own that took some getting used to, but then started to feel like the status quo. I was surprised all over again each time it changed.

Diane came about 8:30 p.m., and I took her into the den to fill her in on the events of the day, where things were holding, and what we could anticipate for the night. I also told her about not crying and why that was important. She listened attentively, gave me a hug, and then went into my mother while I walked Rosa out. In my mind, I was still planning for the night ahead, as though it would unfold much the same way as the day had. But when I went back into my mother's room, I immediately noticed that her breathing had changed dramatically in the two minutes I had been gone. I heard the distinctive sound of the rattle, known as the "death rattle," that is a sign that death is imminent. Diane wasn't familiar with this sound and so didn't know what was happening. She had just been sitting beside my mother talking quietly to her.

In an instant, I realized that there was little time left. I asked Diane to please go into the other room so I could be alone with my mother. I began saying the prayers identified in *Mourning in Halachah* as those that should be said during the sick person's last moments: *Yigdal, Adon Olam, Ana Beko'ach*, and the second paragraph of *Aleinu*. I had marked them in my siddur the day before. After all the waiting, it felt like everything was suddenly happening so fast I could barely keep up. I talked to my mother one last time, telling her how much I loved her, what an incredible life she had lived, and thanking her for all she had given to me and the family. I poured my heart out to her, wanting to send her on her way with as much love and devotion as I possibly could. I opened the window (as I had read in *Mourning in Halachah* 3:25) to make way for the departing soul. She was lying there so peaceful and still. The only sound was her labored breath. I heard her exhale. And that was it. The next breath never came.

I recited the prayers designated in the book for the moment of death.

שמע ישראל ה׳ אלקינו ה׳ אחד — *Hear, O Israel, Hashem is our G-d, Hashem, the One and Only* (one time).

ברוך שם כבוד מלכותו לעולם ועד — *Blessed is the Name of His glorious kingdom for all eternity* (three times in a whisper).

ה׳ הוא האלקים — Hashem is G-d (seven times).

ה׳ מלך ה׳ מלך ה׳ ימלך לעולם ועד — *Hashem rules, Hashem ruled, Hashem will rule for all eternity* (one time).

It was 9:15 p.m., the eighteenth day of April, the seventh day of Iyar.

I called out to Diane and she came into the room and stood beside me. I showed her the prayers we needed to say after the soul has departed. Together we read: "*Hashem gave, Hashem took. Blessed be the Name of Hashem from now to all eternity.*"

"*The Rock! — perfect is His work, for all His paths are justice. G-d of faith without iniquity, righteous and fair is He.*" Then, with Diane's help I tore *keriah*. She started the tear and I completed the rip from my collar to about four inches down on the left side of my shirt. Before she started I said the *berachah*:

ברוך אתה ה׳ אלקינו מלך העולם דין האמת — *Blessed are You, Hashem, our G-d, King of the universe, the true Judge.*

As I stood there by my mother's bed in those first moments after her death, I thought about the *omer* and the specific *sefirah* on which she had died. The last time she had counted was on the eighteenth day. These last few nights, when she was not really able to participate, I had continued counting with her beside me. And now, she had left the sphere of the physical world and begun her ascent. There was no more opportunity for preparation in this world. Whatever she had done until now would have to suffice.

That night was *chesed sheb'netzach*. It was such an appropriate *sefirah* for my mother to leave this world on — "loving-kindness in endurance." *Chesed*, loving-kindness, was her dominant trait in life and it endured under every circumstance, no matter how trying. *Netzach* also means eternity. I felt like that this *sefirah* was reminding me that her goodness was eternal. Even though she was no longer physically in this world, her *chesed* would endure for eternity.

Diane was by my side all this time. Neither of us wanted to move. There was an incredible sense of peace in the room. My mother was gone. That was clear. The essence of her being was no longer with us. She had moved on. Yet her body, in quiet repose, still spoke to us somehow. We wanted to stay with it longer. The expression on her face was beatific. The feeling of awe was palpable.

But there were also a myriad of practical details to deal with. It was already Thursday night, which meant that, G-d-willing, my mother would be buried on Friday afternoon. Being buried Friday afternoon, a person doesn't go through *chibut hakever*, "beating of the grave," a type of suffering that many souls go through in the process of their ascent to Heaven. Burial on Friday afternoon assures direct passage, without suffering. It felt like the timing was a huge blessing. I wanted to make sure that both the funeral home and the rabbi would be available. Not yet wanting to leave the presence of her body, I brought the phone into the room to make the calls. The funeral home told me that the funeral could be at three the next afternoon and offered to check with the rabbi to make sure he was available. They indicated that they would be over to pick up the body shortly. A few minutes after I hung up, I realized that I didn't yet want to part with my mother's body. I had a number of calls to make to let people know about her death and the time of the funeral, and I wanted to at least make the ones to the people closest to her with her body still there. At that moment, I thought I would never see it again and I wasn't quite ready to let her go.

Diane called back the funeral home for me, asking them to please wait another hour or two before coming for the body. I heard her hesitate in response to something she was asked and then I heard her say, "Just because." They had asked why we didn't want them to come yet. Not knowing how to respond, she heard herself say those words "just because." We laughed about it later. It was such an innocent answer. We didn't really have a good reason. We wanted her there with us just because we wanted her there with us. Anyway, halachah requires that someone watch over the deceased at all times, from the moment of death until the burial. The presence of another person in this capacity helps to keep away any forces of evil or impurity. I was happy that we were the ones guarding her body for these first hours. Later, the funeral home would provide someone to watch her.

We went ahead and made the calls to inform people, and then we had some time to just sit quietly. The feeling of awe was not diminished. She had died just as she had wanted to — in her own home, in her own bed, without any medical intervention and with me by her side. Hashem had been so incredibly good to us. He had taken her just as I had prayed He would, gently and peacefully. When I called Rabbi Feldman to tell him he said, "She was taken with a kiss — a gentle separation of the soul from the body — the breath easing away. She didn't have to be wrenched." I was grateful beyond words.

By now, it was close to midnight, and the men from the funeral home came for the body. Diane's first reaction was to spare me the sight of them covering her with a sheet as they placed her on a gurney and carried her from the house. She gently urged me to go in the other room and told me she would get me when they had gone. Not thinking, I started to do what she had suggested. But the second I was in the other room I realized that this was all wrong — of course I had to be there as they covered her and carried her out of the house — and I came right back out. I told Diane not to worry, that I was fine, and that I wanted to be present for this part, as I had for all the others.

I stood in the hallway and watched. They carried the gurney past me down the stairs, flanked on either side by my father's paintings that peered down from the walls on which they hung, seemingly escorting my mother from the earthly home they had built and shared for so many years to their celestial one. As I watched, they positioned the gurney to carry her out the front door and I realized in an instant that if they continued as they were doing, they would end up carrying her out head-first instead of feet-first. Remembering how she had always said that she wanted to be carried out of this house feet-first — her way of saying she wanted to die at home — I quickly intervened and asked them to turn the gurney around. Looking at me a little quizzically, they nonetheless did what I had asked, turned her around, and carried her out feet first.

At that moment, I actually felt a sense of elation. My mother's every request had been satisfied, down to the last detail of how she was carried out. It felt like a triumphant end to a long, hard journey that had been made with grace, dignity, faith, and unrelenting optimism that, in the end, had not been misplaced. We watched from the doorway as they loaded the body into the hearse and drove away. I later learned from Rabbi Feldman that halachah requires a deceased person to be carried out of a house feet-first; only a person who is still alive is carried out head-first. My mother's expression that she wanted to be carried out feet-first as a way of saying she wanted to die at home was probably something she had heard when she was growing up in her religious home in Germany. The halachah was imbedded in the expression without her — or me — even realizing it.

When the hearse pulled away and we closed the door, Diane turned to me and asked, "Can we cry now?" The question startled me for a second. And then, all of a sudden, I realized the enormity of what had just happened. My mother was dead. Diane hugged me and we started to cry. It was overwhelming and, on top of it, there was so much to do before the next day. We took the bed linens off my mother's bed and, as is the custom, removed all the pillows and covered the bed with a spread. The bed of the deceased is left unadorned as a sign that this was her place (*Mourning in Halachah*, ch. 22, sec. 2). Diane started to cover the mirrors, also a custom in the Jewish tradition. Mirrors cause joy and the mourner is forbidden to rejoice or to be distracted by matters of appearance. Also, mirrors reflect images of people, which can potentially draw the soul of the deceased back. I began writing a eulogy to deliver at the funeral. The rabbi had called earlier and asked me to meet him in the morning, so I knew that I had to prepare as much as I could before then. Also, there were people coming in from out-of-town, including my mother's cousin and two of her nephews, who would be arriving early in the day. I sensed that the only quiet time I would have to think about what I wanted to say was now, in the early hours of the morning.

Friday morning, I went over to the shul to talk to the rabbi and then returned to the house. By then, some of the people who had come from out of town were there, and my friends were helping them to get situated in the various places they would be staying. Other friends were arranging for food to be brought to the house for Shabbos. I wanted to look over my notes for the eulogy one more time and just take a few minutes to be with myself. It had turned out to be a whirlwind day and now I felt like I just needed some quiet time to prepare myself for what was ahead. Other than the rabbi, I would be the only person delivering a *hesped,* a eulogy. Though everyone who would be at the funeral knew my mother personally and didn't really need me to describe her, I wanted very much to convey the essence of who she was and what her life was about.

> Delivering a proper eulogy (hespid) is a major mitzvah. Darkei Moshe (section 344) cites the Jerusalem Talmud as saying: 'The deceased knows and hears his praises as in a dream, and knows everything that is said about him until the grave is filled with earth and he returns to the dust.' This is cited by Taz (loc. Cit. Section 1) and the same is found in the Babylonian Talmud, Shabbos 152b.
>
> (*Mourning in Halachah*, ch. 8, sec. 1, fn. 1)

I had delivered a eulogy at my sister's funeral. I remembered how hard it had been to speak and hoped that this time would be different. The deaths themselves were so different. My sister's death was totally unexpected, and it took place in the prime of her life. My mother had been blessed with a long and satisfying life, and she herself had anticipated her departure from this world with a degree of peace. I just hoped I would be able to do justice to all that she was.

Chapter Twelve

I had arranged to ride with the casket in the hearse to the cemetery. The funeral itself was graveside only. My mother had expressly requested a graveside service; she didn't want the gathering at the funeral home, eulogies there, and then the procession of cars out to the cemetery. She wanted the same simple service my father and sister had had, where those attending come to the cemetery on their own and a short service is held by the grave.

Riding alone in the hearse, as the sole surviving family member, I felt the solitariness of the moment. My mother and I were alone, traveling to her last resting place beside my father. She had made it through a long and challenging life with grace and dignity. She had soared through this last test of her illness with flying colors. And now, within the hour, her body would be resting in the grave and her soul ascending to Heaven through that open channel that burial Friday afternoon, before

Shabbos creates. There wasn't another human being in the world for whom this moment was as large as it was for me.

By the time the hearse pulled up near the open grave, many people were already there. Four men helped remove the casket from the car and carried it to the grave. A few people gave me hugs as I made my way to where the rabbi was standing, ready to start the service. I took my place beside him with the casket and all the people in attendance in front of us.

The rabbi began the service by reciting several chapters of *Tehillim*. He began with Psalm 23:

> *A psalm by David. Hashem is my Shepherd, I shall not lack. In lush meadows He lays me down, beside tranquil waters He leads me. He restores my soul, He leads me on paths of justice for His Name's sake. Though I walk in the valley overshadowed by death, I will fear no evil, for You are with me. Your rod and Your staff, they comfort me. You prepare a table before me in view of my tormentors. You anointed my head with oil, my cup overflows. May only goodness and kindness pursue me all the days of my life, and I shall dwell in the House of Hashem for long days.*

Then he recited Psalm 16:

> *A Michtam by David. Protect me, O God, for I have sought refuge in You. You have said to Hashem, "You are my Master, I have no claim to Your benefit." For the sake of the holy ones who are interred in the earth and for the mighty — all my desires are fulfilled because of them. Their sorrows will multiply, those who rush after other [gods]; I shall not pour their blood libations, nor carry their names upon my lips. Hashem is my allotted portion and my share, You guide my destiny. Portions have fallen to me in pleasant places, even the*

inheritance is beautiful to me. I will bless Hashem who has advised me, also in the nights my own intellect instructs me. I have set Hashem before me always; because He is at my right hand I shall not falter. For the following reason does my heart rejoice and my soul is elated, my flesh, too, rests in confidence. Because You will not abandon my soul to the grave, You will not allow Your devout one to witness destruction. You will make known to me the path of life, the fullness of joys in Your presence, the delights that are in Your right hand for eternity.

After that, he recited the prayer from *Mishlei* 31:10–31, *Eishes Chayil*, "A Woman of Valor."

An accomplished woman, who can find? Far beyond pearls is her value. Her husband's heart relies on her and he shall lack no fortune. She repays his good, but never his harm, all the days of her life. She seeks out wool and linen and her hands work willingly. She is like a merchant's ship, from afar she brings her sustenance. She arises while it is yet nighttime, and gives food to her household and a ration to her maidens. She envisions a field and buys it, from the fruit of her handiwork she plants a vineyard. With strength she girds her loins and invigorates her arms. She discerns that her enterprise is good — so her lamp is not snuffed out by night. Her hands she stretches out to the distaff, and her palms support the spindle. She spreads out her palm to the poor, and extends her hands to the destitute. She fears not snow for her household, for her entire household is clothed with scarlet wool. Luxurious bedspreads she made herself, linen and purple wool are her clothing. Distinctive in the councils is her husband, when he sits with the elders of the land. She makes a cloak to sell, and delivers a belt to the peddler. Strength and majesty are her raiment, she joyfully awaits the last day. She opens her mouth with wisdom, and a lesson of kindness is on her tongue. She anticipates the ways of her household, and partakes not of the bread of laziness. Her children arise and praise her, her husband, and he lauds her: "Many daughters have amassed achievement, but you surpassed them all." False is grace and vain is beauty, a G-d-fearing woman — she should be praised. Give her the fruits of her hand and let her be praised in the gates by her very own deeds.

The rabbi said this prayer in Hebrew and explained that it has many layers of meaning but that it essentially extols the virtues of the righteous woman, that my mother surely was. Then the rabbi began his eulogy.

He began by saying, "There is only one way to describe Gusti Millhauser." He asked those assembled, "If I began the sentence with the words 'She was _____' and asked you to fill in the blank, what would you say?" Without exception everyone said out or mouthed the words, "a lady."

"She was a lady," he repeated and then told the story of coming to meet her for the first time when she was already ill and finding her perfectly coiffed and dressed, sitting elegantly in her chair. He figured someone had tipped her off that the rabbi was coming and that she had prepared herself accordingly. So the next time, he dropped in to pay her a visit unannounced and found her the exact same way. "She was," he said, "at all times and in all circumstances, indeed a lady. It had nothing to do with who was coming to visit."

The rabbi then went on to extol her as the best of German Jewish culture, so much of which has been lost to us. He spoke of her genuine interest in people, her enormous generosity, her unwavering kindness, and her endless enthusiasm, all of which he himself felt privileged to experience. There was not a drop of superiority in her, he said. She simply and thoroughly enjoyed life. She had no interest in any honor or recognition. He talked of the ever-present sparkle in her eyes and the almost Dennis-the-Menace-like quality of playfulness, with a hint of mischievousness that those eyes conveyed. He echoed what many others have said, that you only had to meet her once to have a strong impression. "She faced her life and her death with a straight back," he said. "She wanted no heroic measures, and in the end, she was a heroine. In her courage, dignity, and selflessness, she was a model of how to live and how to die."

At the end of his remarks the rabbi talked a little about the exquisite care, love, and support I had given my mother that helped and allowed her to face her death the way she did. And he explained that caring for and burying the dead is called a *chesed shel emes*, a kindness of truth, since it is an act that it is known will not be reciprocated in any way.

After the rabbi finished, I began speaking:

"My mother left very explicit directions that she didn't want us to stand around crying at her funeral. She wanted us to smile, to remember to treasure life and to live each day to its fullest. That's not an easy charge for any of us at this moment, but we'll try to do the best we can today to celebrate her life rather than mourn her death.

"As all of you know, the last five-and-a-half months were an extraordinary time for my mother and me. We were together twenty-four hours a day, seven days a week, under what were often very challenging circumstances. And what I can tell you is that the woman you know, the woman who always had a smile and a kind word for everyone, who had boundless enthusiasm for life, who always looked great and put together, who always was ready for adventure, and who was concerned for others far more than for herself, was right there the whole time. Like everyone else, I marveled at her ability to live and ultimately to die so well. So I decided to try and identify the ingredients, the qualities that had contributed to her remarkable success. Here's what I came up with.

"First of all, my mother focused on what she had rather than what she didn't have. And she had a lot. She was married to the man she loved and adored and who loved and adored her for close to forty years. They were without a doubt each other's best friend. She was able to have two children who she wanted more than anything in the world. She loved to try new things, see new places, and meet new people, which she did non-stop right up to the time she died. For example, a month or so into her illness she decided, with some trepidation since she never liked needles, to try acupuncture. Stacey, who is here today, began treating her, and before long Mom was a pro, able to feel exactly where the energy was moving, and to reap great benefit. And along the way, Stacey and she became friends.

"In that realm too, she had a lot. She had many, many friends and acquaintances who loved and appreciated her. Old friends with whom she traveled through the decades, and new friends she always made along the way. So even though she suffered devastating losses — of her parents in the Holocaust, of my father at a young age, and of my sister at an even younger age — as well as her own bout with serious illness at an earlier stage in her life and all that brought with it, she felt blessed. That is no small feat. Judaism teaches that a happy person is one who is content with his lot. My mother was.

"Second, she focused on others. As you all know as well as me, she was always thinking about other people's needs. No matter what was going on with her, she was always concerned about what was going on with you — even in this last, very challenging, time. The nurse from hospice said to my friend Abby and me when she made one of her last visits this week that she felt my mother was one of G-d's angels. She had never met anyone like her. She felt my mother's kindness and concern so deeply that she told us that she ended up revealing more about herself than she ever had. Apparently, all the other nurses at hospice who paid us a visit felt the same way. Mom was interested in them as she was in just about everyone she met. She was a great listener and genuinely cared. And she was always ready with advice and assistance. She was never interested in dwelling for long on her own problems, even during this last period where almost every day presented a new challenge.

"Third, she loved to learn. She was always taking classes and, as my good friend Diane said, continued a home-study program after she got sick. We home schooled together. She was an avid reader and there was virtually no subject that didn't interest her. These last months, when she could no longer read because of the effects of the medication she had to take, I would read to her. We studied Torah and mysticism together, among other subjects, and she was endlessly enthusiastic and fascinated by what we read. She always wanted to review, to make sure she understood. And she concentrated with the intensity and single-mindedness of a child filled with endless wonder. I honestly don't know how she maintained that level of interest in all that life has to offer for so long and so consistently, but she did.

"Fourth, she knew who she was and what was important to her. She navigated through life with a deep sense of inner knowing about what was right for her. She was always interested in other people's opinions, but never guided by them.

We all saw that clearly just recently, when she made the tough but valiant decision to forgo all treatment and pursue a natural course that, by the way, gave her more time and a higher quality of life than anyone predicted. Rather than spend her last days agonizing through medical procedures, she was able to keep learning and growing and experiencing life right to the end. She truly blossomed in the months approaching her death.

"One card she received while she was sick summed it up well, with a quote that said: 'Life is mostly froth and bubbles; two things stand like stone, kindness in another's troubles and courage in your own.' Well, courage she had — she faced her last days with a strength and grace that can truly inspire us all. The doctor who initially gave her the diagnosis said it very simply — not everyone is as willing as she was to accept when their time has come and to face it so directly and bravely. She lived with grace and dignity and she died that way — to her very last breath, which I should take this opportunity to tell you was as peaceful and perfect as they come.

"She left this world just as she had hoped to, down to the very last detail. As many of you know, her way of saying that she hoped to live out her days and die at home was to say, 'I want to be carried out of this house feet-first.' Last night, when the funeral home came to pick her up, they carried her down the stairs, with my father's paintings looking down on her, and began to carry her out the front door. As I watched, I suddenly realized she was about to go out head rather than feet-first. 'Wait, wait,' I said, 'you need to turn her around.' And they did. At that moment there was almost a sense of elation, that she had been blessed to have her every last prayer answered.

"Our readings recently included books on death and dying and, as one of them said: 'A life well lived; a death full of love.

182

What more can we ask for?' And that's what she had.

"Love, of course, is another ingredient. My mother gave her love to so many, and in these last months, she received all that love back. And while it may have been harder for her to be on the receiving instead of the giving end, she rose to that occasion, too. And slowly, over these weeks and months, she learned to let in the enormous affection and appreciation — the great love — so many people had for her. It astounded me — the endless flow of cards and flowers that poured into the house. I was so moved by what some people wrote that I want to share just a few of the words that were written to her recently, which some of you will recognize as your own:

❖ 'Your spirit is great — gentle and calm.'

❖ 'I can't help but think of your irrepressible spirit.'

❖ 'You are an exceptional lady, loved and honored by so many.'

❖ 'You've always been a very special person to me and I love you very much and you will always be with me in my heart. You're a role model in every sense and my admiration for you is unending.'

❖ 'You are the greatest gift of all.'

❖ 'When I think of you, which is often, I see you radiating love of family and life...wonderful memories I will always cherish — keeping your irrepressible spirit close to my heart.'

❖ 'You are vibrant, fun, and beautiful.'

❖ 'You never felt you were owed anything by the world or anyone. You didn't feel like you "deserved" anything or were entitled to anything automatically so

183

instead of living with an unsatisfactory comparison between what is and your expectations, you made the best of whatever was.'

❖ 'I admire your emotional strength and self-sufficiency.'

❖ 'You had a challenging life and yet your spirit was always so strong. You always had your glass half-filled.'

"That beauty that was certainly there on an outer level, also had a lot to do with the last ingredient I'll mention, and that is her unwavering belief in G-d, that we are totally in G-d's hands, that everything is *bashert* and happens for a reason. She felt herself a Jew in the very cells of her body, and that deep knowing reflected on her face, in the glow that we all basked in. Sunday night, which was the beginning of the big downturn for my mother, when she wasn't able to sleep, I read to her from the book we were then learning together called *Seeing G-d*. It talked about beauty as a divine quality that we see with the eyes of the soul. What we are seeing really is a manifestation of G-d in the garb of whatever person or thing we perceive as beautiful. What we all loved so deeply in my mother, and what everyone who has ever met her responded to, was that spark of G-d that was her soul. And we were seeing that spark through the eyes of *our* souls. And souls are eternal. So, while we mourn the loss of her physical presence, our soul eyes can still find her whenever we want. As one wise man said as he departed this world, 'When I drop my body, I will remain in all who love me. I can never die. Love me and you will find me.'

"So, we'll be loving you, Mom, and feeling your love for us."

When I finished speaking, we began the process of filling

the grave with dirt. Jewish practice is that each of those present puts some earth on the grave. This actual act of burial is the final personal service to the deceased. That was a very powerful moment for me, both as I watched the others in attendance covering the coffin with dirt and as I did so myself. This was it. My mother's body was in that coffin that was now deep inside the earth. The dirt that was being thrown on top was sealing it into its new home, a place that was forever separate from me in this lifetime. Until that moment, it seemed that I was still somehow in her presence, that her soul was hovering around her body and still somehow available to be contacted. With the covering of the grave, something changed. I felt it. I felt the finality. I felt the separation. I felt her soul moving on like I hadn't felt before.

I had some comfort in the recognition that her body was now in repose beside that of my father's, her soul mate and best friend. I also had a fleeting thought at that moment that the timing was perfect. My sister's *yahrtzeit* was a week after the funeral. To me it felt like death was in some way following the pattern of life. My mother and father had this first week — symbolic of the first years of their marriage — alone — and only after that would my sister's soul arrive. My entire family was now safely in the grave, free to interact with each other however that happens from there. They were all now in a realm beyond my ken and experience. I was the only one still in this world, with life left to be lived and work left to be done.

The rabbi's voice brought me back to the moment as I heard him begin to recite the Kaddish.

May His great Name grow exalted and sanctified (Amen) in the world which will be renewed, and where He will resuscitate the dead and raise them up to eternal life, and rebuild the city of Jerusalem and complete His Temple within it, and uproot alien worship from the earth, and return the service of Hashem to its place and where the Holy One, Blessed is He,

יִתְגַּדַּל וְיִתְקַדַּשׁ שְׁמֵהּ רַבָּא. (אָמֵן.) בְּעָלְמָא דִּי בְרָא כִרְעוּתֵהּ. וְיַמְלִיךְ מַלְכוּתֵהּ, וְיַצְמַח פֻּרְקָנֵהּ וִיקָרֵב מְשִׁיחֵהּ. (אָמֵן.) בְּחַיֵּיכוֹן וּבְיוֹמֵיכוֹן וּבְחַיֵּי דְכָל בֵּית יִשְׂרָאֵל, בַּעֲגָלָא וּבִזְמַן קָרִיב. וְאִמְרוּ: אָמֵן.

אָמֵן. יְהֵא שְׁמֵהּ רַבָּא מְבָרַךְ לְעָלַם וּלְעָלְמֵי עָלְמַיָּא. יְהֵא שְׁמֵהּ רַבָּא מְבָרַךְ לְעָלַם וּלְעָלְמֵי עָלְמַיָּא.

יִתְבָּרַךְ וְיִשְׁתַּבַּח וְיִתְפָּאַר וְיִתְרוֹמַם וְיִתְנַשֵּׂא וְיִתְהַדָּר וְיִתְעַלֶּה וְיִתְהַלָּל שְׁמֵהּ דְּקֻדְשָׁא בְּרִיךְ הוּא (בְּרִיךְ הוּא) לְעֵלָּא מִן כָּל בִּרְכָתָא וְשִׁירָתָא תֻּשְׁבְּחָתָא וְנֶחֱמָתָא, דַּאֲמִירָן בְּעָלְמָא. וְאִמְרוּ: אָמֵן. (אָמֵן.)

יְהֵא שְׁלָמָא רַבָּא מִן שְׁמַיָּא, וְחַיִּים עָלֵינוּ וְעַל כָּל יִשְׂרָאֵל. וְאִמְרוּ: אָמֵן. (אָמֵן.)

עֹשֶׂה שָׁלוֹם בִּמְרוֹמָיו, הוּא יַעֲשֶׂה שָׁלוֹם עָלֵינוּ, וְעַל כָּל יִשְׂרָאֵל. וְאִמְרוּ: אָמֵן. (אָמֵן.)

will reign in His sovereignty and splendor, in your lifetimes and in your days, and in the lifetimes of the entire Family of Israel, swiftly and soon. Now respond: Amen. (Amen. May His great Name be blessed forever and ever.) May His great Name be blessed forever and ever. Blessed, praised, glorified, exalted, extolled, mighty, upraised, and lauded be the Name of the Holy One, Blessed is He (Blessed is He) beyond any blessing and song, praise and consolation that are uttered in the world. Now respond Amen. (Amen) May there be abundant peace from Heaven, and life, upon us and upon all Israel. Now respond: Amen. (Amen) He Who makes peace in His heights, may He make peace upon us, and upon all Israel. Now respond: Amen. (Amen)

186

Following the Kaddish, the rabbi recited the *"Keil Malei Rachamim* prayer:

> *O G-d, full of mercy, Who dwells on high, grant proper rest on the wings of the Divine Presence — in the lofty levels of the holy and pure ones, who shine like the glow of the firmament — for the soul of Gittel bas Yehudah Baruch who went on to her world, because people are contributing charity in remembrance of her soul. May her resting place be in the Garden of Eden — therefore, may the Master of Mercy shelter her in the shelter of His wings for eternity; and may He bind her soul in the Bond of Life. Hashem is her heritage, and may she repose in peace on her resting place. Now let us respond. Amen.*

With that the service was over except for one more prayer which some people said on departing:

> "Go in peace and rest in peace and stand up for your destiny at the end of days." *Chochmas Adam, Matzevas Moshe*, par 14. He cites *Ma'avar Yabok:* "The blessing of those who accompany [the deceased] remains with him as an excellent source of protection even after he is buried. This mitzvah is for the benefit and protection of the deceased. Accompanying the deceased, with all the attendant practices, is true kindness, for in this way the soul of the deceased is strengthened in the bond of life."
>
> (*Mourning in Halachah*, ch. 10, sec. 21, fn. 76).

I lingered after the others had moved away. "Goodbye Mom," I said softly. "I love you more than you will ever know. I pray that your passage now will be easy and that you will rejoice in your reunion with all the beloved members of your family. I miss you and am with you wherever it is you are going now. And you are so very much with me. Goodbye."

Chapter Thirteen

J walked away from the grave to the *shurah* — the two parallel rows of comforters facing each other. Almost everyone in attendance had joined the rows. I felt their love and support as I walked between them to the hearse that was waiting to take me back to the funeral home. It is a remarkable experience, this walk between the rows of people who have just shared in the experience of the funeral and who now are turning their attention to me, to let me know that they are with me and there for me in my grief. I looked in their faces as I walked between them. I saw their sadness, their concern, their awkwardness, and heard the thoughts that were in some of their heads. I could feel that for some of them the solitariness of my walk through their rows was painful to witness. They didn't and couldn't know that I was at peace.

For months now I had had the opportunity to think about and prepare for this moment. I knew the depth of my bond with my family from the inside, and I knew that it transcended all of their deaths. They would always be my family. I would always walk in the world with them even if they were no longer physically here. I actually felt a certain strength. I had done what I had most wanted to do. I had seen my mother safely to the other side. Now she lay in her grave beside my father, not far from the grave of my sister. She was with family. She was also with her family of origin — her parents and her sisters who had preceded her in death. At that moment, I didn't feel anywhere near as alone as I looked, walking by myself through the rows of comforters.

The driver of the hearse took me back to the funeral home, where I picked up my car and headed for the house. The others had headed straight back to the house but when I drove up I saw that they hadn't been able to get in because my friend who was supposed to have the key had forgotten it in all the pressure of getting ready for the funeral. It was one of many moments when best-laid plans go awry but somehow, in the circumstances, nobody seemed to care. It was a good lesson for those other moments when the little things loom large. Here, in the shadow of death, very little in the practical realm that wasn't quite right seemed to matter.

The first thing my friends did when they got into the house was to bring out a basin and water for people who had not had a chance to wash their hands when they left the cemetery. Meanwhile, I entered the house and lit the memorial candle that was to burn for the entire seven days of the *shivah*. Kindling this light helps and honors the soul of the deceased. I also found it very comforting, perhaps because the *neshamah* is likened to a flame of a candle. Coming home to the house empty of my mother, whose presence had filled it so fully for so long, was somehow made easier by the kindling of this light. It was as though it brought her *neshamah* back into the space.

By now, the living room was filled with people. In the center sat one lone low chair for me, the only mourner, to occupy. Without even realizing it, I found myself standing around talking to people and avoiding the low chair. It was as though some part of me didn't want to enter this next phase, these days of intense mourning. Less than twenty-four hours before, my mother had still been lying in her bed upstairs and my focus had still been on her care. Part of me wasn't ready to let go, to admit that she was really gone and that the time had come to grieve.

But there wasn't much time. The mourning period had begun when the burial was completed; the remainder of the day counted as the first day of mourning, even though it was only a couple of hours. My friends knew that on this first day I had to sit low and eat the mourner's meal of condolence, called the *se'udas havra'ah*, meal of recovery. That meal, which typically includes a hard-boiled egg, has to be prepared and served by someone else. One reason for this is to show the mourner that others are concerned for her welfare — that she hasn't been left to fend for herself (*Mourning in Halachah*, ch. 14, sec. 1,2, fn. 1).

My friends had prepared a small plate for me that included the egg and some fruit. They knew I hadn't eaten all day and that I wouldn't want to eat much now in order not to interfere with whatever appetite I might have for the Shabbos meal. They gently guided me over to the chair and urged me to sit down and eat just a little something. Though eating was the last thing I felt like doing, I made myself take the plate they had made and eat the egg. People continued to come over to speak to me as I sat there. It was all somewhat of a blur. Part of me knew what I was doing and part of me was on automatic pilot, numb and slightly dazed. Somehow I managed to get through the next hour, and then the house started to clear out and only the few people who were staying for Shabbos remained.

More than enough food had been sent in, so there wasn't too much we had to do to get ready for Shabbos. Still, the preparations were a comfort, a sense of order in my otherwise disrupted life. I welcomed the feeling of *erev Shabbos*, that special aura of *kedushah* that settles on the house as Shabbos approaches. It was time to turn my attention to serving Hashem, to honoring the Sabbath. Mourning continues in private during Shabbos, but is not publicized through any outward, conspicuous practice. I had only been in mourning for a matter of hours before this shift was upon me. I was back sitting in a regular chair and eating the Shabbos meal almost as though the events of the day hadn't happened. But they had.

There was something almost surrealistic about acting in such a normal, regular way when something so out of the ordinary had just happened. I couldn't help but think about how remarkable Judaism is in this regard. It is set up to help us hold the tension between the dimension of life that is ongoing and unchanging and the dimension that is vulnerable to change in any instant. It keeps us connected to the realm of Divinity that transcends all of this world's events, and at the same time heightens our experience of everything that happens in this world. Through its practices and customs it enables us to inhabit heaven and earth simultaneously.

And that's exactly what I felt like I was doing as I sat there at the Shabbos table, with my mother's nephews and cousin from out-of-town and my close friends only hours after burying my mother. I strained to take in the enormity of the moment, going back and forth between participating in the conversation at the table and retreating into my own private reverie. I felt Hashem with me, helping me to embrace the reality of life and of death simultaneously. At the same time, there were moments when I felt overwhelmed. It seemed so big, so much to digest and come to terms with.

All of Shabbos was pretty much like that first *seudah*, a mix of feeling the blessings and grace of Shabbos interspersed with pangs of intense grief and pain. There were visitors during the day, who seemed happy to come over without the restraints of making a *shivah* call. Yet everyone who came was painfully aware of the circumstances and tentative as to how to relate. From my side, I knew my mother had not wanted everyone walking around with a long face after her death, and especially not on Shabbos when we are supposed to be joyous. I tried to share with whoever came the miracle of her passing, all the wonderful things we experienced together during the months of her illness, and the peacefulness of her last moments. People felt buoyed by what they heard, and I was happy to be able to share the stories with them. The whole Shabbos felt elevated somehow. Everyone who came over had that sense as well. I suppose that there is nothing that heightens our experience of life as much as being confronted with death, even a death that occurs in the normal course at a ripe old age.

As soon as Shabbos was over, overt mourning resumed. I again put on the clothes on which I had torn *keriah* and resumed sitting on the low chair. Visits resumed from my friends and friends of my mother, again in the nature of *shivah* calls. The interlude of Shabbos had provided a respite of sorts where, even though much of the talk still revolved around my mother and her death, it was in the context of a Shabbos visit that looked and felt very different from *shivah*. Also, I had gone to shul Shabbos morning, which was the only time I would leave the house for the week. These next days would be far more intense and focused on mourning.

My mother's cousin, Susi, had come from New York for the funeral and stayed on with me a few days. We had a close friendship of our own that had developed when we both lived in Washington D.C. Her presence was enormously comforting. She, too, had escaped from Germany, and she had known my mother for a lifetime. She admired and appreciated her greatly and, at the same time, had always deeply understood me. She realized what an enormous accomplishment it was for my mother and me to have reached such a profound place together. And she was happy for both of us. My mother's nephew George, also born in Germany, had flown in from California for the funeral. He had been close to both of my parents, cherishing and learning from the way they navigated through life. His deep love for my mother had motivated him to make the long trip from California on virtually no notice. His brother, Jules, also flew in from New York. My mother had given so much of herself to them during her life, I could feel them wanting to give back by making the effort to be at her funeral.

Thinking back on those days now, they're a bit of a blur of people, conversations, tears, prayers, and food platters, punctuated by precious, memorable moments. Rabbi and Rebbetzin Feldman's visit is one of those. Hashem somehow engineered it so that at the moment that they came, nobody else was there — a rare occurrence. I felt their care and compassion the second they walked in. Rabbi Feldman looked around my mother's simple little house and, as though sensing the energy there, said almost to himself: "A lifetime of good *middos*." That phrase really captured my mother's essence and touched me deeply. I was grateful he was able to see past her level of observance and appreciate her for who she was. It spoke volumes to me about Rabbi Feldman's greatness. When I told them in more detail about the days leading up to my mother's death, Rabbi Feldman again said, "She was taken with a kiss."

In the course of our conversation, Rabbi Feldman asked me whether I had inherited anything from my mother. A little surprised by the question, I answered that I had and then he told me I needed to make a *Shehecheyanu*. I was stunned. How could it be? The words of that blessing are: *Baruch Atah Hashem Elokeinu Melech haolam, shehecheyanu v'kiyemanu v'higiyanu lazeman hazeh* — Blessed are you Hashem, our G-d, King of the universe, who has kept us alive, sustained us, and brought us to this season. It's usually said on happy occasions, like the start of *yom tov* or when one buys new clothes or other new things of value. Why would I have to say that now, while I was sitting *shivah* for my mother? As it turns out, I actually should have said it at the funeral, but since I didn't know that at the time, I could say it now. The reason is a deep one. A person has to recognize the good even in the midst of something painful and difficult. Anything Hashem sends our way has to be acknowledged. If a death brings with it inheritance, the inheritance has to be recognized and appreciated as a gift from Hashem. With that in mind, I haltingly said the words of the *berachah*. My heart hurt as I did so. I would have given anything to have my mother back instead of the inheritance. But there it was. She was gone and I had to be grateful for what I received by virtue of her passing.

Now that we were talking about halachic obligations, I had a question for Rabbi Feldman. The laws of mourning prohibit a child mourning for a parent to do many things during the first twelve months from the day of burial. Among other things, they forbid one to participate in festive meals, listen to music or play a musical instrument, participate in a wedding celebration (other than the *chupah*), invite others or accept an invitation to a social gathering, buy new clothes, and receive gifts. This is all an aspect of the mitzvah of honoring one's parent. "But," I told Rabbi Feldman, "my mother wanted me to go on happily with my life after she died. She told me more than once that she had lived a full life and was at peace and that she wanted me to be at peace too and to enjoy my life. How does that fit with all of the halachic prohibitions?"

He explained, "Even though your mother was at peace with her death and didn't want others, especially you, to be sad after she died, we still mourn. We mourn the loss of a beautiful human being –– that a beautiful person who was such a blessing is no longer in this world. The particular reflection of G-d that she manifested will never be again. So, while you can be happy and joyous, the first year after your mother's death is nonetheless a serious time and you need to conduct yourself accordingly. That's what the halachic prohibitions help you to do. Also, the first twelve months after burial are a time of judgment for your mother and, even in life, one would not be out celebrating at a time when he knew his loved one was being judged. That's all the more reason to treat this first year seriously."

Listening to Rabbi Feldman, I could feel the deep truth in his words. All the prohibitions which minutes before had seemed like an incomprehensible burden, now felt so right to me. Just thinking of her facing judgment during this first year was enough to sober me and make me want to refrain from doing anything that could even remotely be considered frivolous. That was something we had never discussed, and perhaps my mother had not even focused on that dimension of what was awaiting her. I felt sure that if she had and we had talked about it, we both would have appreciated the importance of following the halachic guidelines for a child mourning a parent and of not rushing into enjoying life as usual. As much as my mother had meant well when she said what she did, I knew that what Rabbi Feldman was telling me was more in alignment with my soul — and probably hers too. As it turned out, his words of wisdom profoundly influenced my experience of mourning in the days and months that followed.

All week long I listened to stories from my mother's friends and my own about this fierce and fine lady whom they had loved and admired. Few knew much about her personal past. What they knew was how she had conducted herself, how she had been there for them, how her strength and courage inspired them, how she had been a source of comfort and wisdom. And how she had always looked so elegant and had never complained. Once again, it struck me as almost superhuman. I marveled, as I had for a lifetime, that there was none of the messiness of life. The suffering, the hurt, the disappointments were edited out. She hadn't spoken of them and so, it seemed, they didn't exist — even though I and everyone else recognized that, of course, they did. But everyone knew her only as positive, upbeat, lively, smiling, enthusiastic, and encouraging. It was finally clear to me that this was not a façade created for the outside world. Any doubt about that had been resolved in these days prior to her death when, despite all odds, she essentially maintained the same demeanor. Even her brief foray into a darker domain had been conducted with a certain grace and dignity.

After a lifetime of trying to penetrate her defenses, I had chosen in the end to honor them and ultimately to admire them. She had remained strong and clear even under the pressure of impending death and substantial suffering. And I had remained by her side, escorting her to the door of the next world in the

196

way she chose to go. Perhaps for the first time I understood that her way of being, that for so long had been my nemesis, was really my inheritance. While it would never define the totality of my existence as it had hers, it certainly could be, and in fact, was, part of me as well. It was a gift she had given me long ago that I had to grow into. I had to become strong enough in my own innate capacities to make room for those with which she had been blessed and had wanted so badly to transfer wholesale to me. My mother was one of the pillars inside of me. Letting myself appreciate her strengths gave me a huge reservoir of resources to draw upon in addition to those I had cultivated on my own.

My dawning awareness about all of this was reflected in the comments of her friends, who saw in me aspects of my mother as well as the ways in which we were different. Even the plumber who had done work for her for decades told me that I was doubly blessed — with everything she had plus all that I had on my own. It was a new and heartening perspective for me that was one of the gifts of *shivah*.

On the morning of the seventh day, I sat for a short time as required, and then Diane came to help me formally terminate the *shivah*. First she said the two verses from *Yeshayah* that are customarily recited: "No more will your sun set, nor your moon be darkened, for Hashem will be an eternal light for you, and your days of mourning will end" (*Yeshayah* 60:20). "Like a man whose mother consoles him, so shall I console you, and you will be consoled in Jerusalem" *(Yeshayah* 66:13). Then she walked outside with me and around the block. Symbolically, this walk represents reemergence into society from which the mourner withdrew during the *shivah* week (*Mourning in Halachah*, ch. 29, sec. 1). For me, it was a mini journey through the past and into the future.

I could feel my shakiness and vulnerability after a week cocooned in the loving embrace of friends inside the house in which I had grown up and in which I had now tended to both of my parents in their dying days. I was glad for the support of Diane's arm linked with mine. The block we were walking around was one I had circled many times as a little girl — running with my sister, on roller skates with my playmates, on my bicycle with my father beside me teaching me to ride. Later, as an adult, I had circled it with my mother when I came to visit and we would go for a walk. And now, this same block was serving as the place for my first symbolic steps into the next and, at that moment, unknown chapter of my life — a chapter that would no longer include my father, sister, or mother. Everything was eerily familiar yet at the same time so different.

When we returned to the house, Diane left for work. I stood alone in the living room and looked around. Now what? *Shivah* is remarkable in many ways, but the one that stood out in that moment was how fully it occupies the attention of the mourner and gives that first week after a death focus and structure that it would never otherwise have. As exhausting and draining as it is, it's truly a blessing.

Chapter Fourteen

For someone who has been a full-time caretaker for any period of time, death brings the added disorientation of losing not only one's loved one, but also one's job. After the death and the *shivah*, the matter of moving forward looms large. I could feel it rumbling inside of me, but at the same time, I realized that my responsibilities vis-á-vis my mother were far from complete. There was much still to do on the practical level and, beyond that, there was the very real work of grieving awaiting me. During the time my mother was dying, I knew she was the one being tested. She rose to the occasion and handled herself admirably. Though it was hard for me, I knew that my test would begin where hers left off. It would be in the days and months following her death when I would be challenged.

While she was dying we were still together. We had our combined strength to call upon, and it was formidable. She set the tone. Her upbeat, positive, fearless stance provided a framework within which I could give the very best of myself. It was that same unwavering position on life that had continually frustrated me that in the end sustained both of us through what could have been a very difficult and unpleasant period. Instead, it was uplifting and inspiring.

Not since early childhood had I joined her so willingly in her reality. And now she was gone. I stood alone in my own reality, changed by the experience of caring for her in ways that I didn't yet understand. There was much to look at, to feel, and to work through before I would be ready to head back out into the world. And there was still much to do on the practical level. I asked Hashem for the strength to do all that I needed to do in the inner and outer realms. I knew that I was blessed to have the time to handle this transition so consciously, something I hadn't been able to do after my father and sister died. And I trusted that, ready or not, this next chapter would grow me in new ways again.

The first thing I had to do was to take care of all the administrative tasks that follow in the wake of a death. The paperwork that tyrannizes our lives doesn't end with the grave. Everything a person has set up for herself has to be dismantled. Credit cards, memberships, and subscriptions have to be canceled. Death certificates have to be sent out to insurers. Accounts have to be closed. Various government agencies have to be notified. And, of course, every company and organization invariably has different requirements as to what is needed. So there are lots of calls to make and letters to write, each one ratifying the death and underlining the new reality that much more. I was unwinding my mother's life, dispensing with all of her connections to the outer world. None of these things had meaning where she was now.

By this time, too, I had received many notes of condolence and contributions in my mother's memory, and I wanted to write thank you notes for them and for all the kindness that had been bestowed during the months of illness and the *shivah*. The thought of doing all of this entirely on my own was daunting. And that was only the beginning. The whole house, stuffed to the gills with decades of life, had to be gone through and emptied out. I wondered how I could possibly do it all. Yet there was no one else. Somehow, I was going to have to tap reserves within me that I couldn't then even feel. The best I could tell myself was to take it slowly, to identify one small thing to do, do it, and then move on to the next. At some point it would all be done.

Telling myself those words reminded me of a story I had heard years before about a boy who had been given a project by his teacher to write a report about all the species of birds in their area. The boy had been overwhelmed by the task. Not knowing where to start, he put it off for days. Finally, shortly before the project was due, he worked up the courage to tell his father his dilemma and ask for help. The father was quiet for a moment and then he put his arm around his son and said to him, "Bird by bird son. That's the only way to do this. Bird by bird."

Thinking about that advice in the context of clearing out my mother's house, I decided to pick one room and start with one drawer in that room. I told myself that all I needed to think about and do for the moment was that one drawer. When it was finished, when I had sorted through its contents, keeping what I wanted and either discarding what I didn't want or earmarking it for disposal by some other means, I would go on to the next. I wouldn't even think about anything besides the one drawer which, of course, seemed very manageable. My body relaxed as I freed myself from thinking about the enormity of the task in its entirety. What was the point? The only way to do it was bird by bird. And that's what I did.

I looked at everything — every photograph, every letter, every scrap of paper. I didn't want to miss any part of the story that might lie hidden in a closet or box. I knew from going through my sister's things after her death, that there is a level of knowing, an intimacy of sorts, that happens in the process of sorting the belongings of a loved one who has died. There is no other time when we have access to all the stuff of a person's life at one time. We don't even encounter ourselves with this level of totality, except perhaps when preparing to move, and then it's easy to just throw things in boxes without really looking at them.

Here was a chance to study my mother's life beyond her relationship with me, beyond her role as mother; to see her world through her eyes. All the things that mattered to her, that she considered valuable and important, were gathered in one place. The books she had read, the music she listened to, the keepsakes she had treasured, the quotes she had bothered to write down, her recipes, the cards she had kept, the names in her address books, and on and on. A collage of her life, and to some extent my father's and sister's, laid out before me. Though sad that my sister wasn't there to do it with me, I felt fortunate that I could take the time to go through it all. There was something healing in the process, some way of reliving and then letting go of the past.

There was also something redemptive. By going through all of my mother's things systematically, I was redeeming what couldn't happen for her with her own mother from whom she was so brutally separated, never to see her or anything of hers again. I had the opposite experience — able to be with my mother as she died and to lovingly go through her things, taking care that each found its right address. This chance for *tikkun* felt like an enormous blessing as well.

My friends who knew what I was doing joked with me when they called, and asked what decade I had been in that day. Especially when I went through all the photo albums, some of which contained photos so old and tiny that I had to use a magnifying glass to get a good look at them, I would feel transported to earlier times and experience them as if they were happening now. There was something comforting about being immersed in the history of my family at the same time that I was adjusting to the reality of being the only member still alive. It was as though I was shoring up my memories, reminding myself of all that had been even as I prepared to go forward without any of it. What would be left of the past would be what lived on inside of me. In a sense, as I was reviewing and culling through my mother's things, I was also reviewing and culling through my family's story. The process was giving me another vantage point from which to view and understand my origins.

But some days the whole thing felt more like a mundane and tiresome task that I couldn't wait to finish. There were so many everyday things to dispose of. Also, my mother had collected things in her life and on her travels that over the years had increased in value. I didn't want to squander assets, yet I didn't want to get bogged down in selling them. Before doing anything, I carefully picked out items to give to her friends and relatives to remember her by. I had done this with my sister's things as well and it gave me — and them — great pleasure. I liked knowing that something that my mother or sister had enjoyed now graced the home of someone close to them. I knew they lived on in all of these people's hearts, but somehow, having something tangible of theirs in all of these places added another dimension that was significant for me.

I also appreciated those of my mother's things that I was keeping for myself. When I would wear a skirt or blouse or jacket of hers, I somehow felt her with me more. That also happened when I would wear a piece of her jewelry. Even some of her *chotchkes* that I used to tease her about and suggest she stop collecting took on new meaning. As I looked at each one, trying to decide what to do with it, I came to appreciate the workmanship that had gone into many of them. There really were some beautiful pieces. I could see why she had liked them, and I surprised myself by keeping more of them than I ever thought I would.

When she had been physically present, none of these things interested me or spoke to me. But now that she was gone, they were a tie of sorts to her and to the home I had known all my life. It was one thing to have a life stripped of all these things while she was still alive and living her life that included them. It was quite another to leave them all permanently behind. I wasn't ready to do that. I realized that in this realm, too, I was incorporating aspects of my mother into myself.

Chapter Fifteen

*A*ll of this sifting and sorting and getting rid of in the material realm was actually mirroring a much deeper emotional and spiritual process inside me. That was the real work of this time. As much as it looked like I was clearing out my mother's house, what I was really doing was the even more challenging task of grieving. I knew that I was at a major turning point in my life — my last parent had just died and I was about to head back into the world alone, without immediate family. I knew from earlier losses that grieving was the bridge from where I was to whatever new life I was about to embark on. I needed to integrate all that I had just been through, to let this deep and profound loss open me to new possibilities. I knew from experience that the pain and heartbreak of loss is not meant to constrict, to diminish us. It's meant to expand and grow us into the next stage of our lives.

As I thought more about it, I realized that in many ways,

life is a continual encounter with ending after ending and moving through to the next opening. And that it is the emptiness that follows the ending that carries us to the opening. We don't need to be afraid of the sensations of lack, the unfulfilled longing, the powerlessness to make it otherwise, the uncertainty about what's to come. They are the waves on which we can ride to new places in ourselves and in our lives.

I thought, too, about the many transitions that are made through loss, through giving up what was. It is actually the first thing asked of us when we're forced to leave the womb. Then there's the baby who gives up the mother's breast to drink from a cup, the girl who surrenders her toys, the young adult who leaves home, the mother of grown children who faces her empty nest. Learning to let go of what was before in order to fully partake of what's to come is a lifelong process. We are continually asked in a sense to say goodbye — to people, places, things, time, feelings, dreams, ages, abilities, events. Everything in this world is finite. So by definition, it has to end, we have to let go. And willingness to experience loss is the key to this core movement of life.

Death, of course, is the ultimate letting go. For the person who is dying, the challenge is to exit with dignity, to accept that their time on earth is ending and that they must leave all that was once dear to them. For the bereaved, the challenge is to separate, to let go of the loved one they lost and to some extent the self they were, to go on with life and still remember. Some days it felt like too much. Just the thought that I would never again see her or talk to her or hear her voice or give her a hug, felt so painful. Especially in the first weeks after *shivah*, I thought at times that my heart would break — but somehow it just kept stretching to hold whatever I was willing to let myself feel. Hashem was clearly helping me, as He had before, to make my way through the thicket of grief.

One thing I thought about was that in losing my last parent, I had also lost my place as a daughter. Whatever duties, responsibilities, expectations, and connections had been anchored in that role were now gone. I felt both the release and the disorientation. Even though I had been living an independent life for many, many years, all of these things had been subtle tethers. Their invisible cords had been part of my orientation.

I remembered when my sister died and I had grappled with the reality that I was no longer anyone's sister. The identity of sister had been with me since the day I was born. Even my birth announcement had been issued in my sister's name. And because there were only two of us, my parents had often said our names in one breath, contributing to our feeling of being an entity unto ourselves. Then one day she was gone. I stood alone. My name no longer rolled together with hers. With her death, I felt like I lost a part of my past, my present and my future. I had no other peer who had lived through our shared history, had grown up in the home in which I grew up, had known me through every turn in the road since the day I came into the world, and had experienced life with our parents from the inside as she had. We had been very close at the time she died and had dreamed of what would be when we got older, the experiences we would share in later life. But all of that was lost the day I walked into her room and found her dead.

Until she died, I hadn't even realized that part of my identity was based on her being there. She had always been part of the background of my life, part of the wholeness of my reality. She was so intrinsically a part of me that I simply took it for granted. I also took for granted the strengths and character traits that were so much a part of her. She had contributed those to my life without either of us consciously knowing it. It's just how things were. Until they were no longer and I realized that I needed to grow those strengths and traits inside myself if I wanted them to continue to be part of my life. That actually became a way of honoring my sister's memory. By acknowledging her gifts and trying to emulate her ways in those areas, I enhanced my own life and made her an indelible part of it.

My mother was even more embedded in my identity than my sister. Fully separating the strands that wove us together over all these years was not going to be easy. Yet I sensed that her death would actually help me to better see her for who she was, independent of me, and to see myself for who I was, independent of her. She was no longer here to be a reference point for my reality, to be a counterpoint to my sense of self. She had moved on to a new world. She was in the midst of an experience that I knew nothing about. That thought would jolt me whenever it came to mind. For, however close or distant my mother and I had been, we always had at least a vague idea of what the other was up to. Now I didn't have a clue. Everything that I was still busy with no longer had meaning for her. She was somewhere else entirely.

Though part of me was well aware of that, there was another part that seemed to be operating as though my mother were still occupied with the stuff of this world. I could sense my desire to dispose of her things in the way she would have wanted. And when the refrigerator in her house stopped working, I initially felt myself drawn to buy a new one from the appliance man she had gone to for many years. I could hear her voice in my head extolling all the benefits of buying from him — benefits that might have made sense for her but really had no relevance to me in my present circumstances. It took a little chat with myself to remind me that she was truly gone, that I should buy the appliance for the house — which at this point was actually my house, not hers — from whomever I wanted. It really didn't matter.

Actually, with her gone, a lot of things no longer mattered. Mothers, perhaps more than anyone, seem interested in the minutia of our lives. Even if they're not available or able to commune with us on the big and important issues, they're often right there when it comes to the little details that even spouses and close friends could often care less about. Had she been alive, my mother probably would have been interested in who I bought a new refrigerator from, even if it was for my house and not for hers. In that way, all sorts of little things were elevated to connective material running between our otherwise separate lives. With her gone, they were relegated to a place of insignificance, which in their own right, was where they belonged. They had acquired meaning only by virtue of their use as currency in relationship.

As painful as the sense of aloneness was from this and other dawning realizations, there was also a newfound sense of freedom and independence. The absence of parents leaves enormous space. It actually surprised me because I had led a very independent life as an adult, charting my own course and not relying on my parents in any way. Yet I was becoming aware of the subtle ways my mother's presence in my life had nonetheless influenced me. I started to realize that there is a whole other dimension of independence that seemingly is only accessible after both parents are gone. I was discovering it little by little for myself. None of my friends had yet reached this stage of life, so I hadn't heard anyone speak of it. It was something of a wonder to me and I felt a little guilty about enjoying my peeks into the possibilities it contained. After all, I loved my mother dearly and I missed her a lot, so how could I be feeling a sense of relief and even excitement about life without her at the same time? It was one of those times when my developed ability to hold the tension of opposites came in handy. I knew that all of those feelings were real and they could co-exist inside me simultaneously.

As a child of a Holocaust family, I was aware that I had carried a heightened sense of responsibility for my parents. I sensed that perhaps this feeling of freedom had something to do with having finally discharged that responsibility. I tried to feel into the subtle sensations of release that I was starting to experience. As I did so, I realized that what was happening to me was part of the story of the Holocaust that is continuing to be written to this day. That story was one I was familiar with not only from my own life, but also from the lives of a number of my clients who also came from Holocaust families. I had seen commonality in the issues many of them were dealing with and often heard the echo of my own experience in theirs.

There is a complicated web woven between the generation of the Holocaust and their offspring. I remembered talking about the impact at different junctures in Second Generation groups, reading about it in the literature and hearing my clients describe it. I realized that this was another such juncture that perhaps many of us were just now getting to — this moment in time when our parents, whose stories were so big that in some ways they dwarfed and enveloped our own, leave this world. I felt myself drawn to reflecting on this bigger phenomenon that was being hinted to in my experience of losing my mother.

Obviously, there were others like me, who had lived their lives wrapped in the long tentacles of the Holocaust and who suddenly would find themselves sprung. I wondered what we as a generation would do with the newfound freedom. Would we be able to honor our parents' memories and all they endured without chaining ourselves and future generations to the fallout of trauma? What would we see as our responsibility to those who came before and those who came after us? And what would we see as our responsibility to ourselves and our Creator? I knew that each generation has its own destiny, its own role to play. And I understood that our parents' experiences and callings, even in circumstances as monumental as the Holocaust, could not substitute for our own. Yet what would that translate to, in the aftermaths of their deaths that would separate us in ways we couldn't have imagined when they were alive? What new chapters would we, the surviving offspring of the Holocaust generation, write in our own stories?

I decided to make time to write about these questions, to really delve into what I had learned over the years from working with myself and other children of the Holocaust. For many, I thought, it might be the first time they could truly feel a sense of their existence in their own right. Somehow, through a process that might remain a mystery, it seemed that children of Holocaust parents absorbed a feeling that their existence, at least in part, was justified as justification for their parents' existence. They didn't feel an independent basis for their existence. Some didn't even feel that they existed in their own right at all.

To their parents, these children were the reason they had been entitled to survive and they made very little, if any, distinction between themselves and them. With their children in the world, these Holocaust refugees and survivors could assuage their feelings of devastation and guilt for all that was lost. Their children gave their lives, their survival, meaning and purpose. This was a life task that preceded the births of

Holocaust offspring, an assignment that was not theirs to turn down. On some unconscious level, these children had lived for that end, to fulfill that objective. They became an integral and essential part of the worlds their parents created, woven deep into the fabric of their parents' lives, leaving them out of touch, to varying degrees, with their own.

I had seen in my healing practice that it took conscious effort for someone with this history to internalize that she had a right to exist, a right independent of the role she played in her parents' life. Each person is not only the child of her parents, but the child of G-d, who contributes the soul that enlivens each body. While G-d very purposely sends each of us into the world through particular parents for soul-related reasons, this doesn't change the fact that each parent and each child exist in their own right with their own soul-work to do. I knew as I wrote these words, that it sounded so simple and basic, but I had witnessed first-hand that for those growing up in Holocaust families, it is not so simple and basic. I realized that after their parents' deaths would be the first time in many of these people's lives that they would stand solely in their own right. They would no longer justify their parents' existence and their parents would no longer justify theirs. What new parts of themselves would they discover, I wondered.

For other Holocaust offspring, this time following their parents' deaths might be an opportunity to more accurately assess the trials and tribulations of their own lives which, measured against the atrocities of the Holocaust, had perhaps seemed more insignificant than they would once the yardstick of the Holocaust was removed. My sense was this time would offer people a chance to achieve new, and perhaps in some ways more accurate, perspectives on themselves, their lives, and what was being asked of them in their own right. I realized that, ironically, many of us with roots in the Holocaust, who often were asked to act mature very early, may just start to break ground on certain aspects of who we really are after our parents die. With their passing, we end the phase of our lives that, at least in part, was given over to their stories, even it if appeared that it was they who gave themselves over to us. From early ages, I and many other children of Holocaust families, sensed ourselves responsible for our parents' well-being at a deep, core level, even as they took impeccable care of us in other ways. We, their flesh and blood, felt their fragility where others saw their strength. We understood as perhaps nobody else could, the empty places inside them, and we tried our hardest to fill them. Their realities were inadvertently inserted into ours. The two became confused in a way that few of us could understand as we lived the hybrid tale.

Now, as they die, the hard work of individuating can be completed for those of us who feel so inclined. G-d is the Master of Timing. If it is now that we are truly coming into our own, I wrote, then it is now that our independent contributions are being called for. Age is not an issue. The soul doesn't know from chronological time, only from the task that it is in this world to accomplish. Once we understand that, we can come further out from under the shadows cast by our parents and step into our own light. Our buried voices can be released, and with them we can send ourselves and the souls of our departed elders soaring.

It was an exciting thought. I could feel something deep inside of me relax as I wrote about all of this. I sensed that much of it was probably also relevant to most adults who had lost both their parents. Though the Holocaust amplified the connections and feelings considerably, the basic work of learning to stand exclusively in one's own right has to be done by everyone who is orphaned. Parents in general are a yardstick of sorts, against which we measure ourselves from the time we're infants. Whether we want them to think highly of us or we don't care what they think, whether we want to be close to them or we want to keep them at bay, whether we perpetuate or reject their expectations — whatever stance we live out in relation to them — they are a factor in the equations of our lives. Even the sheer fact that they are alive puts a buffer between us and our sense of our own mortality. There is still a generation before us; our own deaths seem more remote as long as they are there.

Once our parents die, though, there is no ignoring that we are the next in line. There is also no ignoring that however our parents factored into our measurement of ourselves, the yardstick that they provided is no longer there. We are our own barometers of how we are faring, of the value of our life choices, even more so than ever before. The parental void puts the spotlight squarely on us. It asks us to know ourselves in new ways yet again. It is now up to us more fully than it ever was before to carve out for ourselves lives of purpose, of spiritual evolution and of emotional fulfillment. There is nothing left to expect or to get from one's parents. That may mean that we have to reconfigure our expectations for ourselves, or some of the ways in which we conduct our lives. It may mean that we have to take more responsibility for nurturing and loving ourselves, or at least for no longer beating ourselves up or making unfair demands on ourselves.

The more I reflected, the more I realized that loss of parents is a deepening agent. It puts surface issues in perspective in a different way. It allows us to begin to see ourselves more fully, to see our own outlines against the backdrop of our deceased parents, who are no longer there to influence or be involved with us. There is nothing left in this realm to gain, to lose, to protect, or to defend against. Whatever our situation was with our parents is how it will remain, other than inside of us, where we can always continue to grow and evolve. There are no more chapters to be written in the physical world, only in the world of the heart. It is solely up to us now to come to terms with what was — whether it was great or terrible — and move on from there. We're on our own. And we're free to come fully into our own, to find an even deeper level of self-acceptance and ease than may have been possible before.

The word really is maturity. True — not acted — maturity. Losing both parents brings one to a new level of development, a new level of reckoning with life. In a way, I was surprised. The Inner Torah process I developed and used in my work (and with myself) was all about taking responsibility for oneself, becoming an adult in the true sense of the word, taking care of oneself with kindness and wisdom, and understanding that we, in partnership with Hashem, are charting our own destinies by the choices we make and the ways we behave. It's all about ceasing to blame others, especially parents, for the state of our inner and outer worlds, about releasing our parents, and others, to be people in their own right with all of their strengths and weaknesses and to do the same for ourselves. I didn't realize that as much work as we might do in this direction, when parents are actually no longer alive, there is still another level of independence and autonomy that comes within reach, another dimension of maturity that becomes available to us.

But it takes work. It doesn't happen automatically. I realized that there are plenty of people who have lost both of their parents who don't grow and change from the experience. They get through it and carry on exactly as they did before. I saw it with some of the older people I knew, who didn't have the benefit of the tools for developing awareness and consciousness that were available to my generation. They didn't take the opportunity to step more fully into adulthood when their parents died.

From reading and talking to people, I understood in a deeper way that saying Kaddish is one of the ways that this sort of mindless movement from one chapter of life to another is avoided. In books, articles, and other personal accounts, I saw time and again how for men who spent the year after a parent's death saying Kaddish, there were new openings, new understandings. The enormity of the commitment and the changes required in one's life to meet it were enough to open new doors in the hearts and souls of those doing it. As a woman, that option wasn't available to me, so I was happy to have my own means of paying attention in the days and months that followed my mother's death.

Chapter Sixteen

In time, I finished writing the book I had been working on and began to think about returning to Israel. But it was harder than I thought it would be to separate from Baltimore. This last period of living in America had spoiled me. The religious community in Baltimore was warm and unified. The presence of the yeshivah and Rabbi and Rebbetzin Feldman brought an additional dimension of *kedushah* to the town. There were many learned *ba'alei batim* and lots of learning opportunities for women. *Chesed* was in abundance. Deciding to leave all of that and start over again in Jerusalem was not an easy decision. After all those months of agonizing about when and if I could go back in the early days after my arrival, now I sometimes found myself wondering *whether* to go back.

I had even grown fond of the house — the last remnant of my family — that by then I was living in quite comfortably.

And then there were the few close friends of my mother's, now in their nineties, whom I had started to visit and help after my mother died. It was hard to leave all of that as well. Quite simply, and much to my surprise, I had gotten attached to Baltimore and my life there. It was really quite sweet.

Still, when all was said and done, I felt my soul called to be in Jerusalem. So I began doing what I needed to do in order to return there. The biggest task was emptying out the house that had been my family's home for most of my life and packing a lift. To my surprise, even with the clarity I had about my soul's truth, I was still overcome with sadness. Instead of the usual excitement with which people pack a lift to move to Israel, I was doing it with a heavy heart. I knew that my soul needed to be in Jerusalem to have the opportunity to fulfill the purpose for which it was here. But my heart was clinging to Baltimore, to my family home, to my close friends who had been there for me so totally during these last trying years, to the comforts of living in America where I was fluent in the language and at home with the culture, to the convenience of living a Torah-observant life among fellow Jews who were kind, caring, and considerate.

When I left this time, I would no longer have any family presence in Baltimore, in the United States at all. Having my mother and sister, and later my mother, in Baltimore while I lived in Jerusalem was another of those unseen tethers that had oriented me without my even realizing it. With all of that gone, it felt different again. The move was more real, more permanent, more final. My friends saw how hard it was for me, and at the same time, they understood my need to go. They were kind, supportive, and caring, helping with the packing whenever they could and buoying me with their love.

The day of my flight, I paid one last visit to the cemetery, to my parents' and sister's graves. I had gone there many times in the months since my mother's death. Once I made the decision to go back to Israel, visits to the cemetery felt even more precious, as I knew that soon they would be out of reach. That last day, I arrived ready to say goodbye and saw instantly that the tombstone that extended across the width of my parents' grave was cracked straight down the middle. The crack hadn't been there before and, for a split second, I thought to myself that my mother must have up and left her side of the grave to come with me to Israel. I almost had to laugh. It was such a bizarre thought. But I wouldn't put it past her. With tears and a heart overflowing with love, I said my goodbyes. Leaving three rocks behind me, one on each grave, I then went to tell the man who had made the tombstone about the crack. He also found it surprising. "It's just not something that typically happens," he said.

I returned to the house one last time. Diane and Abby met me there to take me to the airport. Saying goodbye to the family home, after saying goodbye to the family graves, was wrenching. All I could do was hold on tight to my soul's truth. And then I was off.

My friends in Israel were as warm and welcoming on the receiving end as my friends in America had been sending me off. In those first moments after I arrived, as I made my way to Jerusalem, I felt a deep peace come over me. I was where I belonged. But it didn't last. Within a few days, the bottom seemed to drop out. All of a sudden, everything felt wrong — being in Israel, renting the particular apartment I had rented, making my home in Jerusalem. I felt as though I was being pulled back to Baltimore. With every step forward, the force pulling me backward would intensify.

I described what was happening to Rabbi Feldman and explained how surprising it all seemed. "I was so sure that my soul needed to be in Jerusalem," I said. "Your soul does need to be in Jerusalem," he responded, and reminded me that Eretz Yisrael is only acquired with suffering. Apparently, mine was starting within just a few days of my arrival. I felt myself being tested and wondered where I would find the strength to get through it.

Then I remembered one of the great secrets of the Torah. Efforts to ascend in holiness attract the Satan. The *yetzer hara* fights for its life when a person does something significant to come closer to Hashem, to live more fully in the realm of *kedushah*. Perhaps that was the reason for the doubts and second guessing of my decisions. One thing was for sure. I had never experienced anything like what was happening in those days following my return to Jerusalem. I had certainly made significant life choices and transitions before without even a hint of the turmoil I was now encountering. The forces attempting to undermine me at this juncture were stronger than any I had known.

I started going to the Kosel to daven. Every day I walked there and poured my heart out to HaKadosh Baruch Hu. I asked Him to please help me transition back to Jerusalem if that was where I was supposed to be, to grant me *menuchas hanefesh*, peace of mind, in this next chapter of my life. Days turned into weeks and I just kept davening. I started to feel a subtle shift. My distress was no longer so great. Each day it diminished more until, one day, it was gone.

It was about three and a half weeks into my daily davening at the Kosel when I realized that the storm was over. I felt an opening deep inside myself and something settling within me. I was at peace. My whole body relaxed. I felt grounded and sturdy in a way that I had never known before. The war within me had been won by holy forces, which had held me in place through great turmoil. I was astounded by it all and enormously grateful to Hashem. I decided to continue davening at the Kosel every day to offer thanks; I felt so blessed and grateful. And so I did until I reached forty days.

During this last period of davening, my lift had arrived. With renewed strength from the *yeshuah*, salvation, I had received, I was able to single-handedly unpack and set up my home. And this time, it really was a home. With beautiful things from my parents' house and from different chapters of my own life gracing my Jerusalem apartment, I felt a tremendous sense of integration. The pieces of my life were coming together in a new way.

Just about that time, I received a call from a friend of mine in Shaarei Chesed about a *shidduch* she thought sounded good for me. He's a *rav*, she told me, and also an author of *Sifrei Kodesh*. Two weeks later we met. Four weeks later we were engaged. Five weeks after that, the week before Pesach on the exact English calendar date on which my mother had died — April 18 — we were married. The significance of the timing was not lost on us. On the same English date that I had walked my mother home — to her eternal home — Hashem walked me to my rightful earthly home.

Shortly after the wedding, I called one of my mother's close friends, Bobby, to tell her the good news. Then in her early nineties, Bobby was elated and asked me if my new husband had children. "Yes," I answered. "How many?" Bobby asked. I told her the number, *bli ayin hara*. There was a long silence and then she burst out laughing for what seemed to me to be an unusually long time. I couldn't imagine what had gotten into her. When she finally pulled herself together, she said, "I can see your mother, *aleha hashalom*, in front of my eyes as clearly as if she were standing here right now. She would always say, Just you wait, she's going to marry a man with exactly that number of children that you just said!" Bobby continued, "She must have said it to me at least a half a dozen times."

I was hearing this for the first time. My mother had never said any such thing to me, nothing even close. And these conversations with Bobby had taken place long before she became ill. I was surprised and delighted. My mother had her little streak of clairvoyance after all, though she would admonish me from the time I was a child not to fly off to such places. For all I thought I knew about her and her inner world, there were obviously volumes which I would never know. Somehow, I liked that. There was a sense of mystery, a recognition that every soul is so much bigger than any of us can even imagine. It reminds me in my life today that I am only seeing a fraction of even those people to whom I am closest. They are all — we are all — so much more than meets the eye or even the heart. We are vast, infinite sparks of Hashem.

Epilogue

Years after my mother's death, it seems in many ways that she is almost as much a part of my life as she would be if she were still here. My husband feels like he knows her well. Between the stories I tell him of my family and the many times I find myself quoting my mother (platitudes and all!) she feels quite familiar to him. And we both enjoy the things from my parents and sister that grace our Jerusalem home. There is a sense of continuity — physically, emotionally, and spiritually.

Still, when the time came, it was difficult to sell the family house in Baltimore. Though I was already married and deep into my new life, I felt wrenched by the separation. The house was the last significant remnant of my family's past. Somehow, continuing to own it, even though I no longer inhabited it, had served as an ongoing connection beyond my conscious awareness. Yet I knew that it made no sense to hold on to it. It, too, was ready to be released into its next chapter, with a new family to shelter and to give it life. More even than the house itself, I found it hard to part with the many trees and bushes on the property, all of which my parents had planted. One of those trees had been the inspiration for my own profound spiritual awakening as a child, that I described in my book *Inner Torah: Where Consciousness and Kedushah Meet*. For weeks after the sale I was plagued with dreams, showing me the depth of my connection to this last physical anchor from my past. There was still more to do within me to complete the process of letting go.

The test came months later, when my former next-door neighbor called to tell me that the new owners of the house had removed all of the trees. "Everyone nearby was devastated," he told me. My parents had planted more trees and shrubbery than anyone else on the block, and the neighborhood had become fond of them as they grew tall and lush, adding their stately beauty to the street. When I heard the news I felt a sick feeling in my stomach momentarily, and then suddenly it dawned on me. My uprooting was complete. The most treasured, and seemingly permanent, part of my homestead was no longer there. The only place my familial past would continue to live on was within me. By then, the integration of what had been before with what was now was sufficiently complete that I finally felt up to the task. The beloved trees of my childhood found their place inside of me, along with everyone and everything else that had mattered.

Recently, after a very dear friend of mine died, I understood something important about death. As I walked through the painful days of missing her, of aching to see her and hear her voice, I recognized that for a period of time after loved ones die, we are most aware of their absence in our world. Familiar sights remind us of them and we are continually reminded of the pain of our loss. But then, at some point, there seems to be a shift from the horizontal to the vertical plane. No longer does the person seem absent. Instead, there is a pervasive sense that they are around, here with us whenever we want. They seem more, rather than less, a part of our lives, but in a very different way.

At the same time, the reality is that we're here to serve Hashem. Misplaced loyalty to the dead that gets in the way of fulfilling our *tafkid* (Divinely ordained mission) is not good — not what Hashem or the deceased want from us. We need to find a way to remember, to hold our loved ones who have died in our hearts, and still continue wholeheartedly with our own lives.

To do that, it helps to realize that death ends lives, not relationships. As I move forward in my life with my family today and my work, I feel my family of origin with me. Death has not separated us. Instead, what's been happening as time goes on, is that I am seeing, with increasingly greater clarity, just who my parents and sister were in their own right. And I am coming to understand more deeply the dynamics of our family and the ways I was influenced by them. In a sense, I am coming more fully into reality — mine and theirs. There is now unlimited room for our respective truths. I can look head-on at aspects of my family and myself that were harder to see or acknowledge in life. Death makes a different kind of space for them and for me to be truly ourselves. And the love grows even stronger. For, to see the whole of another person — his or her sheer humanity with all its many facets, both wonderful and challenging — is to appreciate more deeply G-d's creation. I can feel my heart soften even more, my mind open even further, and my soul touch yet another dimension of knowing that brings me closer to my family, to myself, and to Hashem. Closer to home.